Praise for *Compassionate Critical Thinking*

"Rabois' innovative approach places students at the center of learning, encouraging deep thinking about themselves and the world around them. A timely antidote to conventional education—and stultified thinking in general."

—Sasha Lilley, host of Pacifica Radio's Against the
Grain, author of *Capital and its Discontents*

"Dialogue has often been an important part of the [Buddhist/spiritual] path, but it does not always receive the attention it deserves. Ira Rabois' book, *Compassionate Critical Thinking*, shows the way to do it, and what it can mean for those who engage in such conversations sincerely and openly. This is what education should be about."

—David Loy, Philosophy Professor, Zen Teacher, and
Environmental Activist, author of *A New Buddhist Path:
Enlightenment, Evolution, and Ethics in the Modern World*

"Ira Rabois has written a straightforward and nuanced guide for anyone who wants to blend emotional honesty with the craft of teaching, based on 27 years of reflecting on his own experiments and discoveries as a teacher. Full of illuminating stories, suggestions, and insights, *Compassionate Critical Thinking* will demonstrate to educators, parents, and administrators that attending to students' emotional responses to classroom materials can lead them to think more critically. This book shows how to do justice to the emotional complexity of teaching and learning."

—Susanna Siegel, PhD, Edgar Pierce Professor of Philosophy,
Harvard University, and author of *The Rationality of Perception*

"Ira Rabois—a 21st century renaissance man—has taught karate, philosophy, psychology, English, Social Studies, and drama to secondary school students for over three decades. Drawing on this wealth of experience—and using illustrative vignettes of his students' voices—he takes us on a journey, showing how he has combined mindfulness meditation, creativity, empathy, and Socratic questioning to engage young people in a rich, collaborative learning process he calls Compassionate Critical Thinking."

—Dr. Dave Lehman, Principal, Lehman Alternative Community
School, Ithaca NY, Educational Consultant, Editor of
Connections, for the National School Reform Faculty

"I am excited to recommend Ira Rabois' new book, *Compassionate Critical Thinking*. As an adolescent psychotherapist, my work focuses in part on assisting patients to gain insight into their internal world, to come to understand their autonomous selves and to be able to articulate this understanding to others rather than simply to act them out. The practices outlined in this book wonderfully integrate the education and psychotherapy processes. They are extremely important, effective, and fitting for enabling a young person to both gain better self-awareness and grounding, and to better focus on the learning process."

—Robert Heavner, PhD, Clinical Psychologist,
Adolescent and Adult Psychotherapy

"I fell in love with Ira Rabois' *Compassionate Critical Thinking* on the first page. As a master teacher of heart and mind, Rabois encourages his students to understand and express their inherent wisdom. Trusting that each child has an important viewpoint and perspective, he guides classroom discussions that lead to self-understanding, clear critical thinking, and compassionate awareness. Any teacher who reads this book and uses its methods will find new inspiration for their students and for themselves."

—Elaine Mansfield, blogger and author of *Leaning into Love:
A Spiritual Journey through Grief*

"Reading this book strongly affirms the role of relationship, both to self and others, in the learning process. Rabois provides a clear path for using mindfulness in the classroom to foster empathy and genuine connection with the material being explored together in class, empowering both students and teacher. The book guides the reader through a process of helping students learn more about themselves and their own learning processes as they make meaningful personal connections to class material."

—Sarah Jane Bokaer, English, Humanities, and Drama Teacher
at Lehman Alternative Community School, Ithaca NY,
and Mindfulness Practitioner

Compassionate Critical Thinking

How Mindfulness, Creativity, Empathy, and Socratic Questioning Can Transform Teaching

Ira Rabois

ROWMAN & LITTLEFIELD
Lanham • Boulder • New York • London

Published by Rowman & Littlefield
A wholly owned subsidiary of The Rowman & Littlefield Publishing Group, Inc.
4501 Forbes Boulevard, Suite 200, Lanham, Maryland 20706
www.rowman.com

Unit A, Whitacre Mews, 26-34 Stannary Street, London SE11 4AB

British Library Cataloguing in Publication Information Available

Library of Congress Cataloging-in-Publication Data

ISBN 978-1-4758-2881-8 (cloth : alk.paper)
ISBN 978-1-4758-2882-5 (pbk. : alk. paper)
ISBN 978-1-4758-2883-2 (electronic)

♾™ The paper used in this publication meets the minimum requirements of American National Standard for Information Sciences—Permanence of Paper for Printed Library Materials, ANSI/NISO Z39.48-1992.

Printed in the United States of America

Contents

Foreword

There is an ever-growing consensus among educators at all levels, K-12 and beyond, that we need to move away from an approach to teaching that simply exposes students to material, passively "covering" as much curriculum as possible, without deeply challenging students intellectually. Students in that environment might be able to repeat material on a test, but both retention and the ability to transfer their knowledge and apply it outside the tightly circumscribed testing environment are low.

We see much better outcomes when students actively engage with the questions they're asked and the material they're learning. The questions cannot be predigested, simply requiring mindless plugging and chugging. Instead, they must be open-ended enough so that the students have to think about different approaches they can take to not just answer them, but interpret and shape them so that they can bring their knowledge and skills to bear. They must be meaningful to them and call for collaborative work and active questioning of their own experiences as well as the material. The students need to navigate the opportunities and pitfalls implied by interacting with other learners who are just finding their feet in the material and, depending on age, as human beings.

When students are intellectually engaged in this way, they become excited by learning. They draw connections between the concepts and skills they are acquiring, connections that improve all aspects of learning. They apply the knowledge they're given not only in the classroom but outside it. They become more aware of who they are and who the others are who share the classroom—and planet—with them. They think more deeply and clearly and become more confident in their abilities.

At the same time, active and open-ended investigation is profoundly scary. You just never know whether an idea or approach to a problem is going to work. Real learning implies risk. In my own teaching at Harvard, I have seen students become more risk-averse, more focused on knowing exactly what the requirements for a test, a paper, a course, a grade are, and then producing exactly that. Many students want to go into a learning situation already knowing at the very beginning exactly what the end results are going to be. But that cannot be learning—that can only be the reproduction of something that has been acquired elsewhere.

An active engagement requires that students be in the right frame of mind. They need to be focused on the task at hand and open to exploring the possibilities and constraints that make up the problem they're solving. They need to learn how to face the discomfort of not knowing. This presents both a challenge and an opportunity to teachers.

Compassionate Critical Thinking is a wonderful contribution to the growing work on this topic. Drawing on decades of experience of teaching and meditative practice, Ira Rabois gives us a toolbox of activities that blend mindfulness practice, philosophy, and cognitive science to help students get into the proper state of mind, and once there, understand the learning process so that they can take ownership of it. He shows us how empathy, combined with a sincere commitment to meaningful questioning on the part of teachers, yields a sincere concern in students for intellectual and social understanding.

Each of the chapters offers sample lessons to show how the different aspects of the approach can be blended. But of course, not all of us will want to, or be able to, teach the lessons as Ira does. Instead, the book invites us to approach our own teaching with the same mind-set that Ira has been fostering in his students throughout his career: to be open to the possibilities he shows us, to understand them deeply, and to adapt them to our own situation. This is a book that requires and repays mindful engagement.

Bernhard Nickel, Director of Undergraduate Studies
in Philosophy and Professor of Philosophy,
Harvard University

Preface

Is there any more vital task for an educator than teaching how to think clearly, critically, and compassionately? Imagine doing this in an effective way that reduces anxiety and increases emotional awareness and prosocial behavior—you could transform education. The method described in this book was developed over 27 years of teaching in an alternative public secondary school. It combines mindfulness, creativity, empathy, and Socratic questioning in a natural process of compassionate thinking. The student becomes present enough to openly face a problem and to look outwards to an object of study and inwards to one's self.

MINDFULNESS, CREATIVITY, AND NATURAL THINKING

Mindfulness is a study of the mind and behavior from the "inside." Mindfulness means moment-by-moment awareness of thoughts, feelings, perceptions, and state of mind. It illuminates how interdependent you are with other people and the world around you: how you influence others and in turn are influenced by them. Without being judgmental, it notices whatever arises as a potential learning event. Mindfulness can be enhanced through relatively simple practices. It can be a form of meditation as well as a quality of awareness. By increasing awareness, it reduces stress and enhances your ability to reflect, focus attention and direct your thinking to make appropriate choices. It increases your sense of presence in the moments of your life.

Teachers and students benefit from learning that the quality of thinking depends on the quality of mental state. If you are distracted, distressed, angry, or you don't care, you will struggle to think clearly. "Consciousness is something we live, not something we have," wrote philosopher Evan Thompson.

Teaching how to bring clarity to the mind is thus part of teaching critical thinking. It inherently engages student interest, reduces stress, and thus improves learning. According to the Greater Good Science Center, mindfulness training improves attention, motivation, and learning in students of all ages.[1]

Compassionate critical thinking uses mindfulness to work with the brain, not against it. When faced with a tough problem or a deep question or criticism, what do you do? How do you deal with frustration and resistance? Do you interpret feelings of stress or discomfort as a message to stop and turn away, or to proceed with more awareness? Do you incorporate such feelings into your process and learn from them? Or when you feel uncertain, do you give yourself time to let the problem incubate, let go of what absorbs you, meditate, take a walk in the woods, sleep on it, and let your brain integrate the material at its own pace? If you do, when you wake up the next day, or finish the meditation, you may have an answer to your question or be able to think more clearly.

These elements, of facing and using your feelings, even frustrations, and letting the mind and heart incubate an answer, are part of the creative process.[2] Creativity is not about the creative artist alone. It is the artist whose mind is engaged, awake, and in relationship with others. There is a "social dimension" to the creative act. The act "works," fits the situation, connects. It is a mental state that reveals relationship.

THE DOMAIN OF THE HEART, EMPATHY, AND COMPASSION

Empathy can mean many things. It is emotional connection as well as recognition that another being, like you, feels, senses, and thinks. The psychologist and researcher on the physical expression of emotion, Paul Ekman, describes three forms of empathy. There is the cognitive ability to read what another feels, as when you see another person and recognize his or her emotion. Then there's emotional resonance, when you add feeling to understanding. You feel and recognize what it would be like to be in the other person's situation and feel a concern for that person—unlike a psychopath who can read feelings but not feel them nor care about anyone else's well-being. When you add caring or loving kindness to empathy, and feel motivated to act to end another's suffering, you get compassion.[3] You don't turn away from sensing another person's distress. You might merely recognize the needs of another and act accordingly, or instead of a focus on yourself, another person's needs fill your heart.

If you are to answer questions and solve problems regarding the world around you, how can you do that without opening up to and taking in others? But the benefits of compassion go deeper. To think clearly, you must think with less bias and distortion from your own habits, likes and dislikes. Research shows that when you practice compassion, you use several sections of the brain, including what neuroscientist James Austin, in *Meditating Self-lessly: Practical Neural Zen*, calls "selfless" pathways.

When you perceive another person, you need to see that person both from his or her position relative to you (which uses dorsal, self-oriented brain pathways) and in relation to other people and objects around that person (ventral, other-oriented pathways).[4] This ventral pathway asks "What is it?" or "What does it mean?" in comparison with the dorsal asking, "How does it relate to me?" Without this "other knowing" you can't perceive. Compassion and many mindfulness practices strengthen these other-oriented pathways. You feel the value and meaning in perceiving others clearly and acting for their well-being. You could burnout on empathically feeling other people's suffering, as people in the healing professions might do. But with mindfulness and compassion practices, you don't.[5]

Another result of increased empathy and caring is more engagement in learning. It is a mistake to expect yourself or your students to ignore their feelings when solving a problem or writing an essay. Did you ever try to think, write, or read about a subject that bores you? Or try to understand what you felt no connection to? It is excruciating. Without feeling, there is little meaning. If you pay attention mindfully, you increase your ability to notice, learn from feelings, work with them as a guide, or let them go.

If you are a teacher who wants to stimulate student learning and increase prosocial behavior in the classroom, one of the best things you can do is act with empathy and compassion with your students. As described in the book *Kids Don't Learn from People They Don't Like*, by David Aspy and Flora Roebuck, when teachers completed a program developing authenticity, solicitude, and empathy, then their primary school students from a poor neighborhood showed more progress in math than other students. The rate of vandalism and brawling dropped and student absenteeism dropped to a 45-year low. The resignation level of teachers also dropped from eighty percent to zero.[6]

Combining Western science with the discoveries of mindfulness practices from different cultures throughout the world provides a method for teaching students how their thoughts, emotions, perceptions, and conscious experiences are constructed moment by moment. Learning about mindfulness and emotion are thus central to understanding how to think clearly. Compassionate critical thinking is reason deepened by empathy and by valuing the welfare of the countless others who inhabit the world with us.

SOCRATIC QUESTIONING AND COMPASSIONATE CRITICAL THINKING

A good question makes a great lesson. Socratic questioning focuses on fundamental questions and reveals theories, assumptions, and the contradictions and holes in those theories. It is dialectical in two senses. One, it focuses on shared and open discussion. And two, once a theory is verbalized or an assumption uncovered, a different or opposing theory (antithesis) is considered and discussed; the problems, limitations, insights, and implications made clear; and a new synthesis is formed.

According to Richard Paul and Linda Elder in *The Thinker's Guide to The Art of Socratic Questioning*, it is systematic, disciplined, and deep. The method works best when both teachers and students ask questions to guide inquiry. For a student to question in a class, there must be feeling, trust and engagement. Educator Sonia Nieto describes how students can be "electrified" by a task on the basis of their own concerns and experiences.[7] When questions are meaningful and substantive and arise from the real situation of a student's life, they evoke the student's intrinsic drive for answers.

For example, after reading a variety of sources on the subject, a class in ancient history discussed how humans, 100,000 years ago, survived despite being relatively puny compared to the more powerful carnivores that surrounded them. One student conjectured the ability to cooperate saved us. Others argued humans rarely cooperate. They were asked to reflect for a moment on these two perspectives in regard to who was responsible for their lunch that day.

Students in this school help serve, cook, and grow the food. At first, there was some resistance to the question. Then the students began to open up, to feel a connection between the intellectual question and their lives, their theory about how the world worked and how they felt—to name the cooks and servers, teachers who helped run the café and taught nutrition. Then farmers and truckers, construction workers who built the roads, and manufacturers who made the plates. Then someone mentioned the farm itself, the earth, the rain, and sun. It didn't take long to include the entire universe in making the lunch.

Notice the process at work here. It started with mental preparation and engagement; students were immersed both in the study of early humans and in their own lives at the school. The question was clear and focused. Students proposed answers. They were questioned mindfully. When you engage the mind, engage awareness of the heart, and vice versa. The result: new learning and insight into interdependence.

The following is a more detailed outline of a process of engaging mind and heart in thinking critically and compassionately:

1. Mental Preparation: Conceptual Knowing and Immersion in the Question.
   a. Focus awareness, define, clarify and engage with the question.
   b. Immerse yourself in the query. Research, collect material evidence, imagine possible explanations, and examine diverse perspectives.

    c. Formulate your own thesis and question it. Formulate antitheses on your own or in a group, analyze the material and various answers, and consider the trustworthiness of sources, truth of propositions, and validity of arguments.

2. Add the Perspective of the Heart and Awareness of Feeling:

    a. Choice requires feeling as well as thinking. Deepen the engagement. Use imagination and empathy to "feel out" or inhabit the question; explore and examine possible implications and consequences of any answer.

    b. To get to new ways of understanding, you need to let go of old ones. Immersion and questioning often lead to frustration and resistance. Reflect mindfully on what you feel as you examine each possible answer, and on your process. Notice if emotions or cognitive biases distort your understanding. Do you need to step back from the material and let it sit?

    c. Integrate the material by stepping back, meditating, dreaming. Let it incubate in your mind until thinking clears and new understanding is reached.

3. Insight, Synthesis and Application:

    a. Synthesize the new insight and create a new thesis.

    b. Translate, apply, question, and test if the new thesis works.

    c. Is more understanding needed? Do you need to reengage the process?

INTEGRATING MINDFULNESS INTO YOUR CLASSROOM

The purpose of this book is to show you how to turn your intentions and goals into a classroom culture of compassionate critical thinking. It is intended for anyone who seeks ways to become more compassionate on a personal level and on a professional level to integrate mindfulness into your classroom regardless of subject area. It demonstrates how a teacher who uses compassionate critical thinking can transform student learning. Mindfulness can help students feel at home in your course, feel more comfortable with you as a teacher, and with other students. It can help you motivate students and engage the critical thinking process.

Over the years, this instructional method was applied across a variety of subject areas—English, philosophy, history, drama, karate, and psychology classes. It was developed in a school where teachers were given space to create a curriculum that fit the specific educational needs and interests of students.

A class can be inspiring like a great story. A great story wakens your mind and heart with a sense of wonder: What will happen next? The reader must relate to the main character in a story, for example, in terms of how they think, or life experiences. Yet the character needs to be different enough to introduce the unknown, the intriguing. The same is true with a lesson.

Students need to feel safe, yet also to wonder, "What strange or unusual people or insights will we read or hear about today?" As students develop a sense of wonder about the class, they develop a sense of wonder about their lives. What bigger mystery is there—what more interesting and relevant story—than the story of your own mind and heart and how they relate you to the world?

Students fear their own story will be a letdown, boring, or filled with monsters. They want to learn that their minds are richer than they believed and that they can face their monsters and make them run. Now that is inspiring.

MINDFULNESS AS A PRACTICE FOR TEACHERS

One benefit of compassionate thinking is you begin to feel smarter in the classroom when engaged in collaborative inquiry than when standing alone in delivering content. You will say and do things that surprise you. So will students. Each weekend you might spend hours planning and imagining, immersing yourself in ways to elicit the critical thinking process. But once you see student faces in the classroom, you will know better what needs to be done, and will sometimes change the strategy for the day to better fit the students on that day. Class dialogue will become mindfulness practice for the students and yourself.

"You can't teach what you don't have," says author and renowned martial arts educator, Hidy Ochiai. A teacher must constantly strive to learn more about the materials that she teaches. This is especially true with mindfulness. If you do not practice on your own as well as with the students, if you are not sincere with yourself, you will not be able to help your students do it. Students recognize authenticity. When a teacher enters the classroom with awareness and genuine caring, students are more likely to do the same. They center on the "inward" immediacy of living and learning together.

NOTES

1. For research studies on mindfulness and education: Emily Campbell, "Mindfulness in Education Research Highlights," *Greater Good: The Science of a Meaningful Life*, September 16, 2014, http://greatergood.berkeley.edu/article/item/mindfulness_in_education_research_highlights.

2. The following book greatly influenced my teaching: Daniel Goleman, Paul Kaufman, and Michael Ray, *The Creative Spirit: Companion to the PBS Television Series* (New York: Dutton, 1992), 18–23.

3. Paul Ekman, *Emotional Awareness: Overcoming the Obstacles to Psychological Balance and Compassion* (New York: Times Books, 2008), 177–178.

4. James H. Austin, *Meditating Selflessly: Practical Neural Zen* (Cambridge, MA: MIT Press, 2011), 21–27.

5. Matthieu Ricard, *Altruism: The Power of Compassion to Change Yourself and the World* (New York: Little Brown and Company, 2015), 51–55.

6. Ibid, 547.

7. Sonia Nieto, "Lessons from Students on Creating a Chance to Dream," in *Shifting Histories: Transforming Education for Social Change* (Cambridge, MA: Harvard University Press, 1995), edited by Gladys Capella Noya, Kathryn Geismar, and Guitele Nicoleau, 6–30.

Introduction

The book is divided into five chapters. Each chapter consists of a series of class lessons that begin with a mindfulness practice, often readings for the class, and include examples of mindful questioning of students. Explanations of the practices and techniques are provided along with sample questions. The first chapter guides the practice, teaching, benefits, and application of mindfulness. It introduces the nature of feeling and the importance of empathy. The practice is simple in structure. The subtlety arises from the complexity of the mind itself. Mindfulness opens mind and heart to clear observation. Learning how to actually see what is there is more difficult.

The second chapter is about knowing yourself and how your brain and emotions structure experience. Understand how the metaphors you use shape the world you perceive. The nature of attention and using stories to structure point of view is introduced.

Emotions and how they are constructed are covered in chapters 3 and 4. Anger, suffering, fear, joy, anxiety, worry, and greed are discussed in chapter 3. And compassion, empathy and love in chapter 4. By learning the components of an emotion, you learn how to manage and use their energy without being run over by them. What is suffering? How do emotions affect thinking? How do you teach emotional literacy? How do you teach compassion?

The fifth chapter spells out the natural process of compassionate critical thinking. Building on the previous four chapters that illustrate the process in classroom vignettes, it includes discussions on dialectical questioning, the nature of truth, as well as how mindfulness develops a quiet, self-aware mind that makes effective self-reflection possible.

This book is structured to do something unique: demonstrate the pedagogical method of compassionate critical thinking. The techniques and tips are meant to inspire teachers to create their own courses using this method.

Students learn more deeply and graduate from school knowing how to engage consciously and more fully with the world, because they have developed the sense that other people and the world around them are not separate but at the heart of who they are.

NOTES ON THE INCLUSION OF STUDENT
VOICES IN THE BOOK

The questions and examples of student responses from classroom discussions included here as illustrative vignettes are not from transcripts. They are distilled from the wide-ranging conversations of students with their teacher in a classroom over many years. They are intended to enable you to better help your students apply the course material to their everyday lives. Hopefully, the account here does justice to the courage, brilliance, joy, and struggles of the students who inspired this book and will enable you to better help your students apply the course material to their everyday lives.

Chapter 1

Begin with Mindfulness

Every moment, every morning, every school year has a beginning. How you begin is critically important. It sets the stage for you to enter and play your part.

Text Box 1.1   Greeting Your Workday.

My first teaching assignment was in the Peace Corps in Sierra Leone. The people of the village where I lived and worked could take several minutes saying hello and taught me the importance of greetings. One day I looked for one of the other teachers from my school. I saw a friend of hers on the road. I went up to her, said hello as if I was in the United States, and then asked if she had seen her friend. The woman took offense. How dare I use her like that! She wasn't there to serve my purposes. I must recognize her, first, with my greeting. Only then could I speak.

Later, when I taught in the United States, I realized I would sometimes get very nervous in the morning as I approached the school building. So I decided to stop, close my eyes for a second, and feel the moment. Take a few breaths. See the trees around me. Observe the building quietly. My nervousness dissolved. It was a way to greet my workday. Then I entered the school.

LESSON ONE: STARTING THE NEW SCHOOL YEAR MINDFULLY

On the first day of school, start with your own mindfulness: What do you feel? By working with your feelings, you gain empathy for your students and yourself. Students are in a situation like your own. When you walk in the school building, do it as your authentic self, not "the teacher." Feel the moment. Let your thoughts and emotions settle. Look at each person, so they feel seen. Think of the school year not as a journey to some other time and place, but into you, here, now.

A classroom can be an extremely stressful, even fearful place—the space crowded, students pressured, teachers constricted in what they can teach by administrators, curriculum, etc. So, signal students—with artwork, quotes written on the board, tables arranged in a rectangle or circle so students can see each other—in this room you can be meaningfully engaged and let go of fear. Play music you think will be calming and slightly new to your students, like the Shakuhachi flute, *Sanctuary*, by Riley Lee.[1] After students enter the room, talk about the question for the day and introduce the mindfulness practice.

You can also use music during most of the mindfulness practices as background to help center the students. In one or two practices, the music itself will be the focus. After a few weeks, ask the students if it is doing its job. Many will find the music relaxing. However, a few students might feel it interferes with their ability to practice mindfulness, so once everyone arrives, turn it off.

Start with an exercise to learn something about your new students. After greeting them, you could give a writing prompt. Direct them to begin a moment of quiet writing while you, too, write. If you ask them to open up, you do it, too. You could ask your students the following questions:

"What do you want to learn from this class? What are your questions?" And possibly: "List things you want me to know about you so I can better help you learn."

It is amazing to watch the students as they work. In moments like this, there is such involvement and earnestness. The flute music helps maintain the sense of calm and quiet. When you start with writing, it lets students know immediately that writing and other forms of expression, their feelings and thoughts, will be very important in this class.

Just like students have to think about what their questions are and what they want to learn, teachers must carefully consider not just what they are being asked to teach but what they feel must be taught. Each person has strengths and weaknesses. Each person comes alive in different ways and is excited by different subjects, topics and means of expression. Every bit of material becomes worthwhile as it relates you to your world, to your lives, and to those of others. And it is this connection you must teach. Often, you have little choice in *what* material you teach; the only choice you have is *how* the material is taught. Therefore, ask questions.

Classroom Scenario

Try playing a Tibetan singing bowl for the class. Ask that they listen to the sound. It is a surprising sound that fills the room without overwhelming it, and disappears slowly, as if leading the mind into silence. Hold up the bowl. Ask, "What is this?" After they reply, ask why Tibetans play it. "It is only a bowl. Who cares about a bowl? It is a beautiful bowl, though, isn't it? Let me play it again."

And ask: "What happens to you when you just listen?"

Listen to student responses. They might say they feel calm, focused.

"So, why focus? And when you focus and all the thoughts are gone, how do you feel?"

One little discussion will start with a simple question and expand until the simple becomes profound. Not only is there an intellectual challenge in this, but a demonstration of how to interact. Students learn to listen to each other and that silence is helpful. Speaking up can be profound. Even within silence, even within the basic and mundane, there is something beautiful and grand.

"Do you know a man named Thich Nhat Hanh? He is a Vietnamese Zen Buddhist monk. In the Vietnamese War, he led a peace movement that spread from Vietnam through the world. He still teaches about peace. He had a practice: whenever you hear this bell, allow yourself to be silent. Just stop, and listen."

Then go around the room and let everyone introduce themselves and share something they'd written in their journal about what they wanted from the class. Listen openly. Student responses are an opening, a tentative statement of trust, as well as a test. Can you hear them? Can you hear what they are telling you about who they are and how to relate to and teach them?

Here are a variety of student responses to this exercise:

- *I want to learn about my emotions, and emotional control.*
- *How can I better deal with anxiety?*
- *I hope my sense of me changes.*
- *How can I scratch from my mind the violence around me?*

Next, you might say, "One reason to take this class is to get to the heart of your experience, to get to the heart of yourselves—wouldn't that be a worthwhile thing to do in school? To do that, you must be engaged in this thing we call a class."

First, ask something serious of your students: Can they commit to confidentiality? "Can you agree to not tell anyone outside this class that x said y? Is that okay? You can share the material, but no naming. Only if we trust each other in this way can we learn in a sincere and open manner. Everyone agree?"

Wait calmly for student responses.

"Secondly, you must do the work. You can depend on the fact that I will do the work. I will always show up ready to learn and teach. You need to do whatever you can. Do the work and you will get something significant from being here."

"Tomorrow, how about we start with a mindfulness practice, with an actual exercise in how the mind works?"

Students don't want to just talk. They want to be convinced by actual experience.

LESSON TWO: WHAT IS MINDFULNESS? HOW DO YOU PRACTICE IT

One purpose for beginning a lesson with mindfulness is that it gives students a personal break, where they can rest in silence. It allows a few minutes to settle into the class and let go of the hallways, other classes, and distractions. Simply getting a break from their quick-paced lives is enormously important for emotional health and clear thinking. Sometimes, students will be too tired or too stressed to do more than just relax for a moment. Let them sit silently if they want, as long as they don't start texting or doing homework. You can't force mindfulness.

Introduce mindfulness in a natural progression. Start the year with research on mindfulness. Instead of just lecturing students about it, have them discern for themselves the benefits of the practice both intellectually and experientially. When you start the year by asking students if they want to talk about the mind and what it can do or also experience what is possible, most students will plead to practice.

Some teachers start the year with a period of silence or simple focus practice and work up to more formal mindfulness practices. Start by asking this question: "Are you aware moment by moment of the thoughts going through your mind?" Then, after sharing viewpoints, ask students to close their eyes and just listen to their mind talk. "Sit where you are and simply be aware of the thoughts or sensations you are experiencing." Students might reply that they have no thoughts, which can introduce discussions about the nature of thoughts and how they arise.

At first, students need to be guided as they practice because it helps them persevere and stay attentive. Later on, you might just tell them that it's time to practice on their own. When you lead the meditation, don't just read the directions to the class. Practice and digest the directions first. Let your voice be calm, clear, and kind. When you suggest any image or direction, know that the mind moves with merely a hint. Do not suggest something that might be misconstrued, scary, or inappropriate.

However, some students will find your voice interferes with their focus and diverts their attention. They may prefer to be given instructions and left alone.

Discover which method works for your class. If you start by leading their practice, after a few weeks, give instructions and let them practice on their own for a day or two and see what happens. Since the practices are short, experiment.

Also, you can only do so much. You are probably not a meditation teacher. You are a classroom teacher who practices mindfulness. Choose practices that fit your particular situation. Here are a few questions you could ask in your own classroom:

- "How many of you have practiced mindfulness exercises or meditation?"
- "How do you know what or how you feel?" Students might reply: *I know what I feel* or *Isn't it obvious?* Respond with questions that direct students to uncover their inner life. Ask: "Has anyone ever said to you that they weren't clear about how they felt? How can that happen?"
- "'Feeling' is often used very ambiguously. What do you think of when you hear the word 'feel'?" You might try to answer this question by intellectual thinking, but the first step in knowing what you feel is to allow *awareness* of feeling.

Your students may come to realize that "feeling" is often used to refer to sensations in the body as well as emotions. There is a close connection between the sense of touch and emotion, as revealed in expressions like "I am touched by your concern."[2] We also use "feeling" to refer to how we value or "feel" about things, as in liking or disliking.[3]

The core of the discussion needs to use questions to reveal course material, including material on how to learn, observe, relate. Suggest the following in order for them to learn how they can begin to assume the power of questioning. "In this class, we need to be clear about what we mean. If you are ever unsure about a word, ask the person speaking, 'What do you mean by that?' or 'Can you say more?'"

Explain to the class that when you talk about feeling, you mean the basic pleasant, unpleasant, or neutral tone of an experience. Feeling is the basic level of awareness. A sensation, however, is that physical quality of hot or cold, squashed or expansive, pins and needles or softly massaged.

Request that students put one hand on the table and ask, "When you touch the table, you have a sense perception. What is it?" Listen to and absorb the different responses, and then ask, "Can you separate the sensation from being aware of the sensation?" This simple exercise can be of surprising import to students.

Any perception is sensation plus awareness. No awareness, no perception. Ask students if any of them perceived the table as gross. If the answer is yes, ask them what gross "feels" like? "Is it a sensation, or a response to a sensation? Is 'gross' in the table or in your judgment of it?"

For clarity of mind, we must be aware of our feelings, sensations, and thoughts and be able to differentiate each of these. Mindfulness educates us in how to be aware moment-to-moment. Ask students if they want to develop such awareness and calm body and mind?

Shifting Theory into Practice

How do you practice? Explain as much of the following to students as you feel is necessary. You could simply say, "Sit relatively straight, eyes closed or partly closed, and breathe through your nose." Or you could go into more detail as explained below.

First, if it's possible, sit on the edge of your chair, so you can keep your spine straight but not rigid. In formal meditation, people often sit in a lotus position or seiza (sitting on heels). In school, this is not always convenient. Place your feet on the floor just under your knees, with heels touching, and toes out at an angle. If you find this difficult, just adjust your feet until you feel comfortable and stable. When possible, give students choices.

Place your hands so your left hand is cupped in the right, thumbs placed to touch at the tip, or nestled so the left thumb is over the right. Or you could reverse it, right hand rests in the left. Some people just rest their hands palm up on their hips. Test which way fits you best. The idea is to hold your hands so tension is neutralized and you can easily stay in one position.

Eyes should be open, closed, or partly open and aimed slightly down. Each eye position has advantages and difficulties. With eyes open, it is easy to be distracted. When you close your eyes, it is easier to let go and relax. However, some people don't like to close their eyes, and falling asleep with eyes closed is easy. Keeping your eyes slightly open, just enough for light to get in and hint at what is around you, can be difficult at first. But if you can maintain the eye position, you maintain focus and not fall asleep.

What follows explains how to lead your students in the practice.

"Let's practice what can be called settling the breath and body. Find a position of balance and stability. Breathe through your nose, both with the inhalation and exhalation. Breathe calmly and, as much as you can, naturally. When we're done, you will hear the Tibetan meditation bowl ring. When you hear it, stop and attend to the sound like we did yesterday. Listen until the sounds and reverberations cease. Then open your eyes, stretch and return fully to the room—awake and refreshed."

"Turn your focus to your breath. Breathe in—feel yourself breathe in. Feel the air entering through your nose. As you exhale, feel the air leaving. That's all you need to do. What is the feeling of simply breathing in—and breathing out? Breathe gently, easily, silently without being artificial. Be present, open. Just do that for a few seconds."

After a few seconds, continue.

"Now, put your attention on your forehead, particularly the muscles around the eyes. Notice what happens in your body as you inhale. As you breathe in, feel what the muscles around your eyes do. Then let go and breathe out. As you breathe in, you might feel the very subtle sense of your body expanding. Can you feel it? Then breathe out."

"Did you notice your muscles relaxing and your body settling? Notice when you breathe in, the body gently expands. As you breathe out, the body relaxes and lets go. This is a natural rhythm of the body. You might notice a calm awareness arise in your mind. You might notice simple sensations in the muscles, of feeling heavy, tense, or neutral. Just notice and then return awareness to your breath."

"Do the same with the area around your mouth. With your attention around your mouth, breathe in. As you breathe out, feel the wonderful, delicious sensation of relaxing, settling down. Your muscles soften and you let go of tension. Then do this with your shoulders. Breathe in, feel the awareness, the expansion; breathe out, feel the settling down, the letting go, the relaxation."

"Any thoughts heard, just let them pass. Allow your awareness to meet the thought, then let it go. Instead of repressing it, notice and bring awareness to it. Then let it go with the next exhalation. Return to awareness of sensations of breathing."

Students will be very calm and, after a minute or so, there will be little movement. Everyone usually participates. Then hit the singing bowl.

"Now, take a moment to write in your journal. Was the experience pleasant, unpleasant or neutral? What were your expectations? Compare your expectations to your actual experience."

After writing for a couple of minutes, ask the class to stop writing and come together. During the practice, notice if anyone was breathing through his mouth, or holding her breath. Some people get into the habit of very shallow breathing or breathing through their mouth. When this occurs during meditation, remind students to breathe through their nose, gently and naturally, and use their mouth only if they have a cold.

This exercise combines basic mindfulness and relaxation. The relaxation developed by attending to the subtle expansion and contraction of the body is fairly easy to do. Before a lesson, especially in the beginning of the school year, relaxation is extremely valuable in aiding the sense of trust and comfort.

Here are some questions to ask after this exercise:

- "How did you feel? Was anything difficult to do?"
  Students might reply that they can't believe they are doing something like this in school or that they feel great. They might say they had trouble focusing or they felt tired.

- "If you're tired, then sleep. Of course, it's better if you sleep at home. Just don't sleep when we're talking together, ok? Mindfulness is about getting to know what's going on. If you're tired, you will know it. If you're happy, sad, whatever, you will know it."
- "How do you keep awake when you're so tired?"
  Many students keep themselves awake during school by using fear or the stress response. Mindfulness gives them other options.
- "Did any of you feel very warm?"
  Students might not realize when you relax, you generally warm up.
- "When you were aware of your breath, did you change how you breathed? When people become aware of the breath, they often slow it down or sometimes speed it up. Allow your breathing to be as normal as possible. You don't have to force your breath in any way."
- "How long could any of you stay attentive at a time?"
  If any students look or say they were anxious, ask: "When people get anxious, how many thoughts do they have?" When you pay attention, you notice more.
- "If you don't notice what is coming at you, can you get out of the way?"
- "Do you feel safer when you're calm and your body and mind settle? Study yourself. Don't just believe what someone else says. Always verify. The inspired mind is very interesting. There's a fury of thought at the beginning. Then distractions fall away. Your mind settles and clears. You feel intensely focused."
- "You might think you need to record your thoughts or feelings. When you practice, you often have the most amazing realizations. You will want to write them down so you don't forget them. But what happens when you write down the thoughts? You lose the clarity out of which the realizations come. The realization might be beautiful and seem very important; but the clarity of mind is why you are doing the practice. The insight is only an expression and derivation of clarity of mind."
- "Which do you want? The actual experience or an idea about the experience? Do you want to be inspired or talk about inspiration?"

LESSON THREE: WHY PRACTICE? DIFFERENT USES AND FORMS OF PRACTICE

Readings for Class Discussion

- Daniel J. Siegel, *The Mindful Brain: Reflection and Attunement in the Cultivation of Well-Being* (New York, W. W. Norton & Co., 2007), 3–22.
- Campbell, Emily. *Mindfulness in Education Research Highlights: An Annotated Bibliography of Studies of Mindfulness in Education.* UC Berkeley,

Greater Good Science Center. September 16, 2014, http://greatergood. berkeley.edu/article/item/mindfulness_in_education_research_highlights.

Compassionate Critical Thinking includes six basic types of practice. In Buddhism and Yoga, for example, mindfulness is part of a larger teaching that includes meditation, wisdom training, and ethical action. Just teaching mindfulness is not enough, if your goal is to fully develop the student's ability to think and act with clarity. You need imagination, empathy and questioning.

The skills developed in the practices ultimately depend on one another. For example, you need mindfulness to concentrate, and concentration to be mindful. Both practices teach how to gently refocus awareness when you drift off.[4] When you act in an unethical manner, your thinking is often confused or you lack information or understanding. The sixth practice—dialogue, questioning and conversation—is used throughout the book.

1. Mindfulness as open, receptive awareness: settling and noticing breath (e.g., deep or shallow, long or short) and sensation (e.g., hot, cold, tense, relaxed), feeling (e.g., like, dislike, no preference), thoughts and images, and what you establish and discern to be true.[5]
2. Concentration: focusing exclusively and pointedly on one object, for example, on the point where air enters the nose or on an image or counting breaths.
3. Visualization: progressive relaxation and imaginative journeying (e.g., to a time in history or a place where you feel safe).
4. Inquiry: after settling the body and mind, introduce a word or topic for the students to explore (e.g., courage, freedom, love or power).
5. Compassion and empathy: for example, visualizing caring for and understanding the emotions of another person.[6] This allows you to view others and the world more clearly and from different perspectives.
6. Group dialogue and questioning: use conversation as an opportunity to practice mindfulness with others as well as to increase attention and develop insight.

Give students a few weeks with each practice. Visualization and inquiry can fit in whenever needed. This book spends only one or two classes on any practice in order to demonstrate a variety of techniques. Each exercise is chosen to fit a specific lesson. Sometimes, the practice is seemingly opposite the discussion topic. A meditation or visualization can take a student emotionally deeper than a rational discussion, so carefully consider the effect of each practice. If you want to discuss hate in a class, first explore compassion. Instead of jealousy, explore gratitude. Instead of fear, explore courage.

Once students have a sense of what courage feels like, they can more easily discuss fear. This method of meeting a possibly hurtful emotion with one that develops a particular strength is close to what is called "skillful means" in Buddhism.[7] It has the benefit of not only preparing the mind for a difficult topic but also teaches how to let go of hurtful emotions by contemplating ones that are more beneficial.

Depending on your subject area, you might want to explore how each type of practice affects the brain. For example, the receptive mindfulness practices use bottom-up, ventral areas of the brain responsible for "other-oriented" perception, objects in relation to other objects, and areas responsible for intuition and insight. The focused, one-pointed practices develop sustained attention and use more "self-referential," dorsal or top-down brain pathways.[8]

A Practice to Use with Your Students

"Yesterday was your first experience of mindfulness, at least in this class. Let's practice a slight variation. To begin, close your eyes, partially or fully. If you leave them open, pick a spot in front of you on which to focus. Or you could close them in a second or two, as you are ready. Take a breath and sense the air as it enters your body."

"What is the quality of the breath? Soft? Refreshing? Is there a taste to it? Taste it. It's amazing, isn't it? Appreciate it. It's the most wonderful thing in the world, yet it's always there. Sense your body expand and come alive as you breathe in. Breathe in awareness. Then breathe out and feel the sensations of the outbreath. Feel the air going out, the letting go, the relaxation."

"Inhale again. And as you exhale, notice how your body settles down, and lets everything go—every thought, concern, word, everything in your mind, let it all go except the awareness of the outbreath. Is there any place in your body where there is discomfort or pressure? Notice the sensations there, just notice. Then feel the breathing in, the expansion. Let the air fill that part of your body. Then breathe out, and let it settle, relax. You are left in a place of quiet and calm. It is like you are now on vacation, a quick vacation. It costs you nothing and you can take it any second that you want it or need it."

"Now take a deep breath. Breathe in the room and stretch upwards. Let your awareness open to the classroom. Breathe out, and come back to the class with full awareness and attention."

Ring the Tibetan bell. Then give students journal questions.

"Did anything come up for you in the practice? Why do you want to practice mindfulness—or to not do it?"

After a couple of minutes of writing, start a discussion with this simple question "Why practice mindfulness?"

The question seems to be meant to reveal if students have read the assigned material and what they understood about the benefits of mindfulness, or what they long for by practicing it. Actually, it is meant to reveal that there can be more to a question than they expect. It is meant to reveal how to learn, especially how to learn something as subtle as mindfulness. It is meant to introduce questions about attention and observation; that how you pay attention influences what you see and the emotions you feel.

Here are some additional follow-up questions/comments to help guide the conversation:

- "What have you noticed so far about mindfulness?"
  If students respond that mindfulness is often "hyped" in the media, ask: "Did you ever notice that when something seems new and different, someone wants to seem new and different by opposing it?" Students might reply that they loved the feeling of taking in air, feeling their own body breathing. Or they might fear this awareness and enjoy learning to let go with the outbreath.
- "How would you define attention?"
  Explain to students that attention is not automatic. It is an active reaching out and the ability to focus awareness. You show you care with attention. You might think you see all that is there in the environment. But your brain must select what it pays attention to. Robert Ornstein, a psychologist and writer, theorizes that instead of thinking of the brain and senses as windows to the world, think of your brain as discarding irrelevant information. You could think of your senses and brain as "data reduction systems."[9] To some degree, you can and do control what you attend to.
- "Imagine you only paid attention to disturbing or negative thoughts. How would you feel?"
  Mindfulness teaches how to pay attention. You become more aware of awareness. Simply, without adding anything, first notice what arises in your mind and body, including what bothers you. Whatever comes up, notice it without commenting. Even if you do comment—"Why did I say that?" "What an idiot!"—Notice the judgment without judging yourself for having it. That is the second step, being aware of your response to whatever arises. "The third is awareness of awareness. 'If you are aware, you can interrupt and let go of whatever arises before it develops any steam.'"
- "What have you found from your research about why practice mindfulness?"
  Students might say it improves their ability to focus, learn, and engage with school material. They might say it improves overall health and reduces stress.
- "If you do mindfulness in order to reduce stress, what happens when you feel the stress in your body? Do you continue practicing?"
  Many students will realize that they usually turn away from what is uncomfortable or difficult.
- "Why practice mindfulness?"

People do it for several reasons. They might do it in order to improve their mood or to focus and think more clearly. But, when meditating, none of those are the reason for practicing mindfulness. "You practice mindfulness in order to practice mindfulness."

- "What do you focus on when you practice?"
The goal is simply to be present and allow awareness of whatever arises. "If you simply allow awareness, your mind becomes allowing, becomes simply aware."

- "If you have ideas and expectations about an experience, can that get in your way? Do you ever judge yourself negatively when an experience is not as good as you think it should be?"
If you practice in order to achieve some expected goal, the expectation itself will interfere with the experience. "Mindfulness is developing what in Hinduism is called 'the witness.' You perceive and notice your perceptions and become present to your life. Judgmental means you have put expectations before experience. Becoming present is the opposite of judgmental."

To practice mindfulness, you need to be open. You need to value it for itself. If not, the mind easily drifts. "To make mindfulness valuable, make the moment itself, this very moment, valuable. This is how you learn. When you don't value something, do you pay attention to it?"

- "How does your focus, or your openness and intensity of focus, affect you emotionally? When you do something joyfully, what is the nature and intensity of your focus?"
Give students enough time and silence to help them discover the links between their mental attitudes and emotions.

- "How do you accomplish a goal? If you don't focus when you take a step, what happens?"
Students may mistake the "now" sensibility of mindfulness for a disregard of the future. Help students realize a mindful focus on the moment can help them plan ahead. Ask them to share one of their goals. A popular goal for many adolescents is purchasing a car. Ask them why they want to purchase a car. They might respond they want to be able to get around, to go places. They might joke about impressing people. Upon further questioning, they discover they want to be accepted or feel free. With mindfulness, you know the real goal. Only if you know the real goal can you address it.

To encourage a short review of the class, invite students to ask questions with this prompt: "If you had the opportunity to ask anyone we read or talked about a question, what would it be?" Let students share a few responses before ending the discussion.

Text Box 1.2 A Practice for Setting and Meeting Goals

Tell your class, "Let your body settle down. Close your eyes partially or fully and notice your breath. With your inhalation, notice any feelings, thoughts, sensations, or images. With your exhalation, let go of the images and return to awareness of the breath."

"Allow any thoughts or images to come to mind of any goal you want to achieve. Is there a goal, a need, or drive that you have? What goal stirs your heart or awakens your soul or gets you through the day?"

"What is it about this goal that motivates you? Do you want this for your own good? To help others? Just ask yourself the question and listen for an answer. Feel the energy within the goal, the passion."

"Visualize achieving this goal. Hear, feel, or picture it. Notice where you are, what you're doing, as you achieve the goal."

"Test it. Notice any thoughts, feelings, emotions which arise in response to the thought or image of achieving the goal. What might the consequences be of pursuing and achieving this goal? How does it affect the people you know? The world? Does the goal feel right? If so, continue. If not? Let go of the goal and turn your attention to noticing your breath, or listening to the sounds around you."

"If you decide to continue, let come to mind the steps you need to take to achieve your goal. What actions will you take when you leave this chair? Do it in your mind so you can do it in reality. Imagine acting fully, with determination, to achieve what you set out to achieve."

"Now, as you breathe in, turn your attention to the room. As you breathe out, open your eyes and look around you."

You could also use a brainstorming technique, especially if you only have limited time. For example, if you want students to form learning goals in your class, ask them to write freely and without editing on what they want from your class. Tell them you will read only what they decide to show you. "What do you yearn to know or be able to do that this class could help you develop or explore? What skills or abilities could this class help you strengthen?"

LESSON FOUR: MINDFUL SPEECH

About the fifth or sixth day of school, after saying hello, ask students a follow-up question. "Did anyone try the mindfulness practice at home?"

It's difficult for people to take seriously the recommendation to make it easy and do it for only two to five minutes, at first. There must be something in American culture that turns attempts to better understand yourself, or decrease stress, into more stress and a burden. Let mindfulness be fun and natural. After a while, your body will ask for more.

Pick a time of the day where you have a natural ongoing activity, like after you wake up, or when you come home from school, or before eating. The morning is a particularly good time. After you get up, do some stretching and exercise, then practice. When you feel fresh, it is easier to focus. Even two minutes will make a difference in your life. A teacher's life, or a student's, can be extremely hectic and full. You can't add minutes to your day but you can deepen your moments.

Over the school year, you can utilize several different types of mindfulness practices. At home, for yourself, pick ones to do that feel easier or more appropriate for you. People will often practice one exercise for years. This next practice will start out as previous ones, but then switch to something different.

The Practice

Begin by requesting that students close their eyes partly or fully in order to settle down, relax, and focus their attention on the whole breathing process. "Be present, open. Allow awareness to settle within. Notice any sensations that arise, where they're located, and the quality—do you sense tension or heaviness, heat or cold. Just allow yourself to notice. Breathe into the area—then as you exhale, notice your body relaxing slightly and return to awareness of the breath."

"Any sounds heard, just let them be sounds. Any thoughts, just let them be passing thoughts."

Take your time leading the practice and let it flow gently. You want students to be able to listen to their own minds more than your words.

"Notice any word that arises. Notice if there's a feeling attached to it, any images or meanings. We usually think with words. Words are artifacts of a culture. An English word could go back to Middle English or Old English, and possibly back even further to Greek or Latin. It could go back before that, to earlier Indo-European or into the mists of history, to the Paleolithic art caves, to painted symbols and the very first words uttered or the first sounds that humans made."

"Every word we speak has a trail behind it thousands of years long. But do you feel that age? Can you feel, now, that connection? Imagine: countless humans before you have spoken every sound you make. Every time you speak, thousands of years of history and pre-history speak through you. Sit for a moment with that sense of depth to the words you speak."

After you ring the bell, invite students to stretch and come back to the class fully awake and energized. Ask them to briefly write about their experience.

After two minutes, get the attention of the class and ask, "In what ways are you this moment in history?"

Hold up an object like a woven basket, a trunk or large envelope; if you can get one, use something beautiful, like a Tibetan, Native American, or African wooden basket for them to visually study and use as a metaphor for a word.

"This is from Tibet. What do you think it is?"

Wait for responses.

"What might you carry in it?"

After discussing these questions and answers, tell students, "Some questions turn your thinking on, others turn it off. Let's do the best we can to try for the former, not the latter. Feel free to ask any question that comes to you that feels real and honest. Go ahead and doubt." Help them to understand that by doubt you mean to question and inquire into the nature of things. But you also need faith in your own ability to learn and think.

"How might a word be like a basket?"

Some students might suggest a word is a basket for concepts or for naming things. For others words are nothing without a person to give them meaning. Students might argue words are merely self-expression; they are baskets you construct to contain your own meanings or they mean whatever you want them to mean.

You can explain that if meaning is all about you, the speaker, assigning shared meaning becomes a problem. If meaning is established entirely by you, how could you ever communicate? The hearer—the person you are speaking with—would also make his or her own meaning out of your words. Would you want this to occur? How could you check that the other person understood what you said? Would you be locked into yourself, unable to communicate? Is speech solely about self-expression? Can you have communication without communion?

Many students wrestle with such questions. Since understanding anything involves subjective experience—your own brain or mind—how then can it be "objective?" Subjective experience, for many people, means the opposite of "objective knowing." But, how can there be an objective truth without a subjective experience—or a subject experiencing it?[10]

Explain that sometimes a person speaks and you lose sight of the reality of their past actions or the situation you are in. They might tell you they love you when their actions say something else. Words are only one aspect of a person's speech. Context and circumstances convey meaning, too.

Ask students to sum up how a word can be like a basket. Explain that words and baskets are both creations needing people, both speakers and listeners, even an imagined listener, to animate them with meaning.

Remind students that once they summarize what they heard and checked if they heard correctly, they can ask clarifying questions: "What did you mean? When you said it, what did you intend to happen? What reasoning and information did you use in your thinking?"

LESSON FIVE: THE HERO'S JOURNEY

Today's class will be on the quality of awareness you bring to mindfulness and being a hero in your own story. Greet students and begin the class by saying: "Today, let's go a bit deeper into mindful awareness." You can ask:

- "Why focus on the breath? What have you noticed so far?"
- "Is there ever a moment when the breath isn't there for you?"

Tell students: "It is so ever present you might take it for granted." By making something as basic as breath stand out, you make your whole life stand out. Paul Ekman said, in a taped discussion with Daniel Goleman,[11] as you practice mindfulness of the breath, you become more spontaneous yet aware. If you can become aware of this basic automatic process, you can become aware of other largely unconscious things that you do, like those involved in emotion.

Many of us do not breathe well. And when you use the breath to help calm yourself and focus, you don't need to go on a vacation in order to relax. Your breath can be your vacation. If you're at a meeting or taking a test, you can't bring out your teddy bear or do a dance in order to calm yourself. But you can breathe. Practicing breath awareness can turn whatever you do regularly and deeply—dancing, karate, art, running—into a meditation.

The Practice

Tell students, "Now, it's time to sit up and let your body settle." Give the students a moment.

"Turn inwards to your awareness of your own breath. Imagine yourself as this open inner space and let your awareness gently fill that space. If or when anything arises, allow your awareness to go there, to just notice, feel, and hear it. It might be a sensation, like sensing yourself sitting on the chair. It might be a thought, a sound, or an emotion. Just gently notice—and then let it go."

"Notice especially your response to whatever arises. When some thought or sensation comes to awareness, what do you feel like doing? Is it easy to just notice and let it go? Or do you jump in the middle of it or push it away to hide it in a fog of confusion? Whatever arises is just a sensation, just a thought, or memory. It passes. Notice what happens when you simply notice and let it go."

"In simply noticing lies a calm that is rare, that can allow you, life, to just be itself, nothing more is needed, nothing missing. Allow yourself to just be. Allow mind to be simply allowing."

Ring the singing bowl.

After a moment, ask students to record in their journal any thoughts or emotions that came up for them during the practice. Then bring the writing to a close. You can ask:

- "Do you ever get lost when practicing mindfulness?"
- "Was there a moment when you forgot what you were doing? If you're very focused, you can hold attention steady for a few minutes. Then you get lost and suddenly realize you have spent the last few minutes someplace else?"

Listen to responses. For most people, this happens frequently. Sharon Salzberg, an author of several books and teacher of Insight Meditation, describes this as "a golden moment" when you realize your mind has drifted off.[12] You remember to remember. You realize, "Hey, I drifted." So what do you do when that happens? Students might say:

- *I get down on myself.*
- *I attack. I get angry at myself, feel guilt, or regret things I did, or wasn't able to be.*

"Instead of embracing the self-judgment, see if you can embrace the awareness. You're aware right now. This is a golden moment. This is what you want to be, aware, strong, and insightful. People tell themselves, 'What an awful meditator! I lasted five whole seconds before having a thought. What is wrong with me?' Or: 'Wow—everyone around me is so quiet. They must be so much better than I am.'[13] Anybody feel that? Raise your hand if you had one of those thoughts."

Most students will raise his or her hand.

"In that second when you realize you are lost, you are found. If a judgment arises, great—note it, and move on. Be open to yourself, kind. The fact that you notice it is perfect. It is normal for the mind to jump around, wander, talk to itself and get lost. It is this 'coming back' without self-judgment that is the most important part of mindfulness practice. Tune in to yourself—then attune to others. Once you harmonize with yourself, you can harmonize with others." Notice the stillness in the classroom.

Ask students what they have learned so far about what mindfulness is. Possible student responses include:

- *Sitting quietly.*
- *Paying attention.*
- *Listening to yourself.*
- *It can get boring.*
- *It is harder than it appears.*
- *It clears my thinking.*

Then ask your students, "What helps or hurts your practice?" Students might say:

- *I have to be more patient and more accepting of myself.*
- *I have to stop feeling that I must, automatically scratch when I itch or check what other people are doing.*
- *I get judgmental because I never know what other people think about me. I judge myself so I can beat others to it. I can get judgmental about anything.*

Mindfulness helps us understand how to trust and how to answer questions as honestly as possible.

We will soon discuss in detail how attention is not only where but how you place your awareness. You have to experiment with how to monitor and modulate your attention moment-to-moment. Sharon Salzberg gave a good example of how monitoring works. When at a store, on line at a cash register, do you see the cashier as a "machine with arms" or as a vulnerable, feeling being?[14]

You have to notice and acknowledge, not just label. Not eliminate the breathing person with a concept. You need empathy. Just like words are a dance for two, so is checking out of the grocery store. Each moment, realize what is going on and bring yourself back. It is not passive. And when you have this interest in each moment, you make better choices.

Alan Wallace, a meditation teacher and prolific author, said mindfulness can be "the engine of transformation." Let's examine what that might mean.

Ask student to sit back, relax. "Close your eyes for a second. Take a nice breath. Think of a hero. Let an image come to mind of someone who is a hero or heroine for you. Just picture him or her or hear his or her name. When you have someone, open your eyes. Who came to you?" Record the students' ideas and then ask what makes these people heroes. Student responses may include:

- *They battle evil.*
- *They fight against oppression.*
- *They risk even death or loss. They put a cause, or maybe other people, first, before their own safety.*

One of the greatest books for understanding literature is Joseph Campbell's *The Hero with a Thousand Faces*. Campbell outlines a basic pattern that appears in myths throughout time and place. The pattern repeats in religious stories, Jesus Christ being tempted in the Desert, the Buddha facing the demon Mara under the Bodhi Tree. These all involve heroism—but also transformation.

Ask students: "Did any of your heroes undergo a transformation?"

Students might mention that Nelson Mandela, in prison, had to overcome his anger in his fight to end apartheid—and later, to push for reconciliation. They might discuss real people or fictional ones and give reasons for their viewpoint.

"One mark of a hero in mythology is the opening of both the heart and mind. How many of you have dreamed of being a hero or heroine?"

Practically everyone has such a dream. The call to be a hero or to start on an adventure can take many forms. The Buddha's enlightenment or the destruction of the ring of power looks exciting and wondrous from an outsider's perspective. But from the perspective of the "character" in a story who does not know what will occur, it can be frightening. Discuss with students:

"The hero must venture from the safe and known worlds into the unknown. Both Frodo Baggins and the Buddha at one point leave home and enter a deep forest, the forest of the unknown. The hero must dive into the belly of the whale or sneak into Mordor. You must face the bully in the cafeteria. In this way you discover faith in yourself. You do not know what will result, but you do it anyway. Out of action, transformation comes."

"Will you adventure into your own mind? Will you bring yourself back to the moment to face whatever arises? You are the hero who shouts to the world, 'I can do this. I can face monsters and make them run.'"

LESSON SIX: USING IMAGINATION AND VISUALIZATION TO TEACH

Visualization is a natural capacity of the mind. It can be defined as "the conscious, volitional creation of mental sense impressions."[15] To go beyond the superficial meaning of language we use mental imagery. When you read fiction, or daydream, night dream, or remember something, it is easy to notice images running through your mind. But it is not always obvious how you use imagery in possibly all of your thinking. Visualization develops imagination.

You can do visualizations on your own or be led by others. You can directly use visualization for examining evidence, finding solutions, revealing hidden attitudes, clarifying, reviewing or synthesizing material, and gaining insight. The process described here is not mindfulness; it is very different from the practices described in earlier lessons. It strengthens the ability to create and apply imagery. It helps students be more relaxed and focused in class. It directly connects course material to student's lives and so provides intrinsic motivation for learning. With enough experience, you can do such practices in about ten minutes.

The method begins with progressive relaxation and then proceeds to a mental journey or story. The story has a beginning that takes you out of your regular world, proceeds through adventures to a catharsis, and then returns you home. The relaxation section will last two to four minutes. Unlike mindfulness, students can sit back or rest their head on the desk in front of them. You can play calming music in the background, for example by Stephen Halpern or Carlos Nakai, but not the music you use for mindfulness. You can center attention first on the feet and work your way up or start at the forehead and work your way down.

Before you begin, tell the students what topic you will be exploring. The following is a sample, 20-minute visualization with directions for teachers for a high-school English class, on the main character, Sinclair, in the novel *Demian*, by Herman Hesse.

The Practice

"Today, we will meet Sinclair in a new light, as we are first introduced to him in the novel, *Demian*."

"When you are ready, sit back and relax. Assume a position that is restful, comfortable and that you can stay in for five minutes or so. Close your eyes now or in a moment or two, when it feels right. Then put your attention on your forehead. Calmly, breathe in, taking it nice and easy; then breathe out. As you breathe in, can you feel the subtle sensation of your forehead expanding very slightly? Just notice it as you breathe in. Then, as you exhale, notice how your body naturally relaxes, settles down. You might settle more into the chair or feel heavier or warmer."

As a leader, you need to keep your voice calm yet natural. Relax. You are teaching a relaxation method. Pace yourself so you introduce a new image or question just after the previous image has formed for your students.

"Move your attention to the muscles around your mouth. As you breathe in, the area might expand a little; simply notice it. Then, as you breathe out, relax, settle down, let go. Then, move your attention to your shoulders. You might find it easier to notice the effect of breathing on your shoulders. Breathe in and feel the expansion. Then, just let go as you breathe out. Notice how your body relaxes even more deeply as you exhale. Your shoulders might drop. Do you feel any warmer, heavier? Just allow yourself to relax."

"Now, allow a flower to come to mind, any flower will do."

If not a flower, pick something that you think will be considered safe, familiar, and of interest to your students. A tree? A quilt? A butterfly? A stone? An animal? One reason I use a flower is to get the mind ready for something more complex by starting with something simple. This simple experience can be great fun. However, always remember that when people are relaxed and trusting of you, their minds will move instantaneously, at a mere hint.

Some students expect one thing, like a rose, and get something different, like a dandelion. It is important that there are no wrong flowers. In some cultures, specific flowers, animals, or colors have a meaning.[16] This can be an interesting topic for research. For now, just notice and relax with what comes.

In teaching social studies classes about primal cultures and religion,[17] students can visualize first a flower and then an animal. Visualizing an animal can be revealing and exciting. Early humans, as in the art caves of Lascaux, France, extensively portrayed animals with remarkable detail and aliveness. Humans, if portrayed at all, were stick figures, except for part animal, part human, or shaman figures.[18] Early humans obviously felt very connected to these animals. Most students even today easily bring to mind an image of an animal.

"Just notice what flower comes up for you. It might be one you know or have seen at your home. It might be one you imagined or read about. Either way, it is fine. What shape do you see? What colors? Sometimes, you will simply see the flower. Other times, your mind will give you words that describe a flower. What words describe it? Just notice what comes to you. Is there a fragrance that comes with the flower?"

"How big is the flower? Notice how delicate it is. How does the flower attach to the stem? What color is the stem? What is its feel, its texture?"

The first time you lead a visualization, just do this much. After you've done this a few times, students will need less time to relax. Use mostly simple questions to help students develop detailed, concrete images. As much as it makes sense, refer to multiple senses. Transitions are important and require sensitivity to how students take your words.

"Behind the flower is a beautiful path through a forest. Sinclair will soon emerge in the distance, from down the path. Can you picture him? What words come up for you about him?"

Here are some sample questions you could use to go further with the visualization. Use those that best fit your goals. Remember to make the visualization clear and concrete.

"Notice how he walks. Does he stand straight, stride, slouch or look calmly around him? How tall is he? What color hair does he have? How is he dressed? What is his facial expression? When you see him, what is your response? When you hear his name, do any feelings arise?"

"Are you happy to see him or upset with him? If Sinclair were a flower [or an animal] what would he be? Does he remind you of any other literary characters? Is he like you in any way? Is there someone on his mind? Who? Do you want to tell him something? What might he want to say to you?"

Return attention to the classroom gradually. Think of it as coming home from the journey. Proceed in reverse order of how you left, but in less detail.

"Now, say goodbye to Sinclair. Remember you can return here any time you want. You can remember anything you want that happened here. Once Sinclair turns and walks down the path, notice the flower, its shape and color. Then notice your breath. With each breath you take you can allow more and more awareness of the room, of your body position. Feel the weight of your body on the chair or your hands on the table. Can you hear any sounds? The music? Other people in the room? Move your fingers. Wiggle your toes. As you take a deep breath, gradually sit up. Open your eyes. Stretch. Notice the room and how it feels to be here."

Eventually, you will be able to simply ask the students to relax, close their eyes, and settle down. Then proceed to the visualization that ties to your class material.

After the exercise, always process the experience with a journal prompt or a small group or whole group discussion. The process will hopefully lead right into the heart of the lesson. Ask students:

- "How was that exercise? Were you relaxed?"
  Listen to responses. Some students might respond that they fell asleep. Assure them that is fine. Students will often process the experience like a dream. Most students will find visualization calming, restful, yet intellectually challenging.
- "Did you get a flower, and an image of Sinclair?"
- "What flower came to you? If you'd like, share with us the name and color of the flower." Go around the room letting students share the flower and the color.
- "Name one thing you learned about Sinclair."

This type of exercise can be used with very diverse groups, books, and topics. If a student says that nothing came to them, go with it. It's fine. If you sense something is bothering the student, talk one on one. Everyone is different. In one class of mostly middle school, hyperactive boys, many of the school staff thought the students would never be able to calm down enough to do the exercise; they were wrong. The students loved it. They relaxed and images came readily to mind. At least once a week after that, they asked to do a visualization.

The Practice for a Social Studies Class

How does critical thinking utilize imagination? Consider how students might answer the following questions in a class on ancient history or human evolution: "Why did early humans create so much art?" Or maybe, "Why did they do any art?" Students often reply, they did it because it was fun. That answer needs to be questioned further. Students need to read about and empathetically immerse themselves in the world of ancient humans.

"What is familiar to you today that was totally lacking back then?" Imagine, a world without any buildings, vehicles, electronic technology, etc. One form of Paleolithic art was extensive wall paintings in caves in Southern Europe, Africa, Australia, and other places. In France, for example, some of the caves were extremely difficult and dangerous to access. Access involved crawling through long, narrow tunnels. Why paint in such inaccessible, dangerous places? Their lives were dangerous enough.

In a class on the history of human ideas, students decided to research, in small groups, various aspects of how the cave painters lived: their food, religion, other species populating the world back then, tools, the origins of language. A group of five or six studied the paintings in detail and then reproduced the art on the walls of a rarely used stairwell of the school.

One day, when the work was complete, this group had the other students line up outside the stairwell, and one by one they entered it. It felt like a cave. The only sound was the music of a flute. The only light source was a series of small lanterns placed near the painted walls. When all had entered and sat down on the cave floor, the students were led in a visualized journey into what being in the caves might have been like. Then the student-artists discussed the paintings.

The students and teacher created the activity together. It was fun. Most still remember the experience. It enabled the class to feel engaged and develop a more in-depth perspective. They could then analyze evidence, evaluate theories, and derive their own conclusions.

This type of activity is not limited to history or English classes. In a science class you could journey through a cell, the orbits of electrons, or the carbon cycle. In social studies, imagine a society without racism. Critical thinking is not just logic or problem solving. It requires imagination.

NOTES

1. Other musicians you can use: Nawang Kechog, Carlos Nakkai, Ronnie Nyogetsu Seldin, and for piano, Liz Story. Use the same music consistently in order to associate peaceful music, calm mood, and the classroom.

2. David J. Linden, *Touch: The Science of Hand, Heart, and Mind* (New York: Viking, 2015), 3.

3. Joseph Goldstein, *Mindfulness: A Practical Guide to Awakening* (Boulder, CO: Sounds True, Inc., 2013), 81–83.

4. Evan Thompson, *Waking, Dreaming, Being: Self and Consciousness in Neuroscience, Meditation, and Philosophy* (New York: Columbia University Press, 2014), 38–39.

5. Goldstein, *Meditating Selflessly*, 121–129.

6. James Austin, *Meditating Selflessly: Practical Neural Zen* (Cambridge, MA: MIT Press, 2011), 44–45.

7. Goldstein, *Mindfulness*, 102–103, 235–236.

8. Austin, *Meditating Selflessly*, 44–45.

9. Robert E. Ornstein, *The Psychology of Consciousness* (San Francisco, CA: W. H. Freeman and Company, 1972), 19.

10. Albert Low, *The Origin of Human Nature: A Zen Buddhist Looks At Evolution* (Portland, OR: Sussex Academic Press, 2008), 20–24.

11. Paul Ekman with Daniel Goleman, "Knowing Our Emotions, Improving Our World." *Wired To Connect: Dialogues on Social Intelligence*, More Than Sound Productions, 2007.

12. Sharon Salzberg, "Mindfulness In Education" (presentation, Omega Institute for Holistic Studies, Rhineback, NY, 8/14/11). I recommend Sharon Salzberg, *The Force of Kindness: Change Your Life with Love and Compassion* (Boulder, CO: Sounds True, Inc., 2005), 17–28.

13. Ibid.

14. Ibid.

15. Patrick Fanning, *Visualization for Change: A Step-By-Step Guide to Using Your Powers of Imagination for Self-Improvement, Therapy, Healing, & Pain Control* (Oakland, CA: New Harbinger Publications, Inc. 1988), 2.

16. Ted Andrews, *Animal-Speak: The Spiritual & Magical Powers of Creatures Great and Small* (St. Paul, MN: Llewellyn Publications, 1997), 1–19.

17. Huston Smith, *The World's Religions: Revised and Updated Edition of The Religions of Man* (New York: HarperCollins, 1991), 365–383.

18. Gregory Curtis, *The Cave Painters: Probing the Mysteries of the World's First Artists* (New York: Anchor Books, 2006), 182–185.

Chapter 2

How Does the Brain
Shape Experience?

The human brain remains a mystery despite so much scientific study of it. Scientists like Christof Koch, chief scientific officer of the Allen Institute for Brain Science, have called it "the most complex object in the known universe."[1] It is so complex and powerful that it is difficult to realize what our brain *is*.

If you say to a class that the brain is more powerful than any computer, don't be surprised if students argue vociferously against you. It might sound to them like make-believe. Yet, think about it. It is difficult to comprehend the radical connection between brain, mind, and perceived world. Try to imagine all the things going on inside you every second the brain coordinates—staying upright, processing sense information, growing new cells, fighting infections, keeping the heart pumping, lungs inflating, skin breathing, stomach digesting, etc. Even the web of interbrain signals is too vast to count. You perceive a world and don't realize that the beauty or ugliness you see is largely a creation your brain makes possible.

WHY STUDY THE BRAIN?

This book provides only a basic introduction to a subject as complex as the brain and how it shapes thinking and emotion. Students often resist discussing material that sounds like "self-help." To teach about emotion, you need to walk a delicate line between getting too personal and too academic. Neuroscience is a "hard" science. It can provide intellectual maps that can serve as metaphors to help you understand why you act, feel, and think as you do. For example, students are often reluctant to let go of emotions like anger. If you study the neuroscience of anger, you are not giving "self-help" tips. By studying the science, students recognize for themselves that just "letting off steam" might actually increase, not reduce, the anger they feel.

LESSON SEVEN: TEACHING NEUROSCIENCE WITH POETRY AND METAPHORS

Readings for Class Discussion

- V. S. Ramachandran, *The Tell-Tale Brain* (New York: W. W. Norton & Co., 2011), 3–23.
- "Life. 126," ("The Brain—is wider than the Sky") Emily Dickinson.
- Jeremy Hayward, *Letters to Vanessa: On Love, Science, and Awareness in an Enchanted World* (Boston, MA: Shambhala, 1997), 22–38.

This lesson is structured for an English class but could be applied to social studies or science. How can you best understand the brain? Students might think that the study of the brain is an academic, irrelevant subject, or a magical one uncovering a depth of life previously hidden from view. The questions you ask set the tone. Make your first questions essential, relevant, deep, philosophic, even moral, and you, in turn, will get such questions from students. How do the metaphors you use influence what you focus on and perceive? In what ways do the images you use of the brain affect how you feel about yourself? What does metaphor reveal about the brain?

The day before this lesson, engage in a short pre-reading discussion on the poem by Emily Dickinson, to arouse interest and help students understand the context of the reading. This discussion might include the historical situation, her family, how her poetry challenged some of the common assumptions of her day, and how the imagery she used introduced important questions about the brain.

Ask the class to think in advance about what ways the brain might be like the sky. Ask them to sit in the outdoors and, for two minutes, look up and observe the sky before reading the poem. Poetry or any literature is a record of the inner life of a person. Reading and discussing it can develop empathy in the reader and understanding it is assisted by mindfulness and empathy practice. Using poetry to introduce material in a science, history, or psychology class can add a refreshing depth to the discussion.

The Practice

A class taught by Hidy Ochiai on using imagery in meditation inspired the following practice. Ask students to settle themselves so that they can hear and

Text Box 2.1   Neuroplasticity and the Usefulness of Discomfort.

"Can you be open to everything?" I ask to begin the class.

"Why not?" says Eli.

"Didn't you say some things are distractions?" Germaine asks.

"Aren't there evil people and evil ideas?" urges Alex. "I don't want to be open to evil. I feel very uncomfortable thinking of being open to evil."

"If you are practicing mindfulness and you notice discomfort, what do you do?"

"Be aware of it," Alex says.

"Yes, exactly. And then?"

"We're supposed to return to the breath. But that's not so easy," says Alex.

"True. It's one thing you're learning to do. You're learning that discomfort will pass, depending on where you put your attention and how you think about it. Is discomfort bad or wrong to feel?"

"No, I think it's not bad, but it feels wrong. I don't like it," says Alex.

"If you don't feel it," I ask him, "will you ever learn from it?"

"No."

"Discomfort can be useful. It's useful that you notice the discomfort of evil. If you didn't notice your discomfort, you would not realize it is telling you to stay away from something. Discomfort actually gives you a power and control that you could not have otherwise. Sometime, we'll need to talk about what you mean by 'evil.' But for now, do you desire more control? I'm sure you want to trust yourself and your sensations?"

"Yes, of course," he replies.

"Scientists used to think that the human brain only developed up to a certain age and then neurons started to die off. No new ones were formed.* Now, we know about 'neurogenesis.' The brain can grow new neurons throughout life. There is also 'neuroplasticity.'" The class then discusses the different meanings of "plastic"; in this context, it means that neuron connections adapt and change.

"The brain changes. We change. So trust that. There is a sense of relief in knowing, 'I can change.' Now, let's practice trusting and verifying your experience."

Note

*   Ramachandran, *Tell-Tale Brain*, 28.

feel their breath. "Just breathe. Breathe in, and feel the opening, feel the in-breath. Breathe out, and feel yourself settle into the process of breathing. Let your body settle down and be at ease, with awareness. Just be here."

"With your next breath, allow your awareness to flow through your body. Feel it—vast and open, like the sky. Imagine the sky on a clear day. What is it like to view the sky? We usually get so caught up in the concerns of the day that we don't look up and see the vastness that opens before us. Look up at the sky. Feel its immense, almost incomprehensible openness and spaciousness. It's quiet. Even when the wind blows, the sky is quiet. Imagine you are like the sky. Instead of feeling crowded or rushed, you feel vast, spacious. When something comes up, your mind can be spacious, vast and open like the sky. Breathe in that spaciousness. When you breathe out, rest in the vastness of mind."

Ring the singing bowl. After students return attention to the classroom, ask them this simple question. "How was the meditation?"

Some students might reply that they lost their concerns in the sky. For others, the sky might be too big, at first, to take in, until they relax and let go of their concerns.

"Do you ever feel crunched, squeezed by ideas, a mood, or pressure?" Allow students to share their experience.

"When you picture the sky, your mind has the opportunity to expand and open. Stress can feel like you are crunched, pressured. Relaxation feels spacious. Visualizing sky can provide a calm openness. Use a visualization of the sky in your mind when other practices do not work for you."

When a class curriculum allows you to study the brain, ask students for their questions. You can expect some of the following questions to come up:

• Is it true you use only ten percent of our brain?
• If the brain is so powerful, how come people mess up so much?
• What are the limits of the brain?
• How much neuroplasticity is there?
• Can you actually feel what others feel?
• Could or should computers be added to people's brains to enhance memory or other abilities? Is mind different from the brain?

Not all of these questions will be answered in this book; however, you are encouraged to discuss them with students and explore ways by which students can find answers to them. Different areas of the brain will not be considered in detail here, either. A list of sources to study the brain in a secondary school class will be provided.

Break the class into groups of three and ask them to complete the following two tasks.

• List metaphors about the brain that are included in the poem.
• Answer the question: "How can the brain be wider than the sky?"

After working in groups, a whole class discussion can begin.
"What did your group say about how the brain can be wider than the sky?" Allow the different groups to share.
"Should Emily Dickinson speak of mind, not brain?" Student responses may include questions as well as theories.

• *Is the brain a part of the body, and the mind something else?*
• *The mind is just another way of talking about the brain.*
• *The mind is something besides nerve tissue. Maybe mind is the experience of the brain?*

The biggest unknown in science and philosophy remains the question of what is mind. Daniel Siegel, Professor in Psychiatry, researcher and author describes how medicine and science lack a consensus definition of mind. He defines mind as "a relational and embodied process."[2] By "embodied" Siegel means the mind is part of a whole physical being. "Relational" means the mind is not isolated in its skull shell but exchanges energy and information back and forth with everything in the universe. However, some neurobiologists have other theories. They think, "The mind is just cellular activity." A computer scientist referred to the brain as "an operating system."[3]

Students will notice that some metaphors imply that the brain and mind are not alive, but more like machines. If you conceptualize the mind as a clock, as it was in the Middle Ages, or a computer, then it's not alive,[4] and it needs a clockmaker or programmer. But if you think of the mind as alive, or as the consciousness of the universe, it's easier to feel connected and it's more difficult to harm other people or the environment.

The metaphors you use shape and provide a context for thinking. Linguist George Lakoff and philosopher Mark Johnson argue that "the way we think, what we experience, and what we do every day is very much a matter of metaphor." Yet, we are not usually aware of our conceptual system.[5] Mindful awareness of our thinking as well as intellectual analysis is crucial for improving how we think. It is fascinating for students to consider how metaphors give our thoughts shape.

The number of atoms in the universe is ten followed by eighty zeroes. The human brain has approximately 100 billion neurons, plus other cells. The tracks of neuron fibers in the human brain, unlike earlier hominids, are folded. To explore what this means, ask students to stand and form a line. Have the line twist in and around so that students are drawn in close to each other.

After students complete the exercise, discuss it. "Which configuration allows more connections?" Listen to responses.

The folds of the brain allow the neurons to form connections upon connections. Each neuron in the human brain can connect with one to ten thousand others. The number of possible connections in the human brain is thus ten followed by one million zeroes, that's one million billion synaptic connections.[6] That's more than the number of elementary particles in the universe.[7] It is difficult to comprehend the radical connection between brain and universe. What does such a mass of highly interconnected tissue, especially one highly interwoven with the rest of the universe, make possible? It weaves not only "us" into everything, but also everything that comes with "us," including our metaphors.

Short Practice

Tell students, "Here's a new image of the brain. Sit back, close your eyes, and imagine a jewel, one with many facets. Imagine each surface is clear so you can see inside it and yet shiny enough to reflect whatever comes near to it. Other jewels surround it. Now imagine seeing in the first jewel the reflection of another one that's nearby. What happens? Notice the infinite reflections of jewel reflecting jewel."

"Imagine there are almost innumerable jewels. A beam of light hits one and bounces around to each and every one. Each jewel has inside it the image of the other. Notice that instead of seeing separate jewels, you see only light, one light shared by all."

"This image is from India. Hindus and Buddhists call it the Jewel of Indra and use it as a metaphor for reality. It is very similar to how some quantum physicists might describe reality.[8] Everyone, now open your eyes and return to the class. The brain might or might not be as interconnected as the Jewel of Indra. But with such a mass of interconnections, can we even understand yet what such a mass of tissue can do?" Give students a moment to take that in.

LESSON EIGHT: THE GEOGRAPHY OF THE BRAIN

Suggested Readings for Discussion

- Rick Hanson, *Buddha's Brain: The Practical Neuroscience of Happiness, Love, and Wisdom* (Oakland, CA: New Harbinger Publications, Inc., 2009), 5–38.
- Daniel J. Siegel, *Mindsight: The New Science of Personal Transformation* (New York: Bantam Books, 2010), 14–22, 50–58.

How does the organization of the brain help create your experience of a vibrant world? In a class where you can study the brain in some depth, have students read the two sources cited above as well as do Internet research. They can immerse themselves in the subject.

In such classes, you can divide the class into five or six small groups to become "experts" in a specific section of the brain and then introduce and teach the material to the whole class. Assign questions for students to answer on their subject. Encourage them to be creative in the presentation—make movies, link material to their life, create illustrative experiences and visuals.

The exercise can take several class sessions. Each group must make sure every group member understands the material and contributes to the discussion. At the end, the class reviews the process and the material provided by the groups. The sections of the brain to research could be the hindbrain, and the four lobes of the cortex, the frontal, parietal, temporal, and occipital. You could include the somatomotor and somatosensory cortex. Do the emotional brain together afterward. At a minimum, assign four questions for each group to answer.

1. Where is the part of the brain located?
2. What are major divisions of the section?
3. List and describe the functions of these areas of the brain.
4. Implications: What important lessons about your own behavior can be derived from the study of this area of the brain?

Mindfulness, inquiry, and visualization exercises can be used to introduce, teach, and help students remember material.

The Practice

Tell students, "Today, we will continue our study of the geography of the brain and what it can teach us about how we experience life. Let's first explore imagination, creativity and why the brain is the way it is."

"First, allow yourself to get settled. Maybe close your eyes and turn attention inwards to your own breath, to your own sensing of the world and yourselves. Let your awareness rest lightly on whatever comes up in your mind and goes away. When anything arises, allow your awareness to notice it. It might be a sensation, like feeling yourself sit on the chair. It might be a thought, a sound, or an emotion. Notice—and let it go. Allow your mind to simply observe."

"Now, imagine you have the ability to alter all human brains. What would you want this new brain to be able to do? What would you change or add to yourself—or to all humans? How would you improve humanity? Let it come to you. Feel, picture, or hear your creative ideas."

"Then consider if you made this alteration, what else might change? How would this affect other aspects of human life? What implications of the change can you imagine?"

"Now, notice your creativity. You were able, in just a few minutes, to create pictures, feelings or words. The ability to create is always there, in mind, ready to help, to spring into action. It's amazing, isn't it? You can imagine situations so easily and readily. Allow yourself to be aware of how easily you imagine. Then, rest for a second in appreciating that ability."

Ring the singing bowl. Ask the class to write in their journals.

"What arose for you in the practice and how did you respond to it?" Wait a few minutes to give them time to write. "Did any ideas or images come to you about how you'd change the brain?" Give everyone the chance to share their answer to the first question before you go to the second about implications.

Students often mention being less violent or less wrapped up in ideas, less greedy, more accepting, empathetic, loving, and creative. One or two students might say they would change nothing. A few might admit they would want a great increase in their own intelligence or physical ability. Would crime and wars decease? If they did, would the human population increase too rapidly? If we are less caught up in our ideas, would we be more able to imagine solutions? If we were less greedy, would we cherish our lives as much? Is there a possibility of a balance between extremes built into the brain?

The human brain evolved over the 3.5 billion years of life on this planet.[9] It can be conceptualized as divided into separate sections, each with different but possibly overlapping functions, some of which are relatively unique to humans. (See figure 2.1 for a diagram of the outer layer of the human brain.) Major human activities such as thought or emotion are controlled by more than one brain section.

The oldest section of the brain is the "hindbrain" which evolved before there were even mammals. It is located in the back, just above the spine.

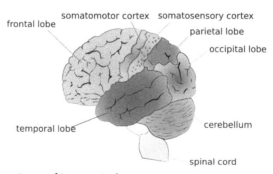

Figure 2.1   Outer Layer of Human Brain.

It includes the brain stem, cerebellum, and other areas, which regulate basic functions, like the sleep-awake cycle, breathing, and balance.[10] Paul MacLean, a brain surgeon and former head of the Laboratory for Brain Evolution and Behavior, theorized three stages of brain evolution. His theory is a useful conceptual guide, although it is no longer considered accurate. He called the hindbrain the "reptilian" brain because he thought this was the kind of brain reptiles had.

The next section was the "early mammalian brain," also called the "relational" or emotional brain. It is located in the middle of the brain and includes such areas as the amygdala, hypothalamus, hippocampus, and thalamus. The last is the cerebrum, and its outermost layer, the cortex, MacLean called the "new mammalian brain." The cortex is divided essentially into four lobes or areas. At the back, there's the occipital lobe. On the sides are the temporal lobes and in the front is the frontal lobe. On top, behind the frontal, you have the somatomotor, the somatosensory area, and then the parietal lobe. The whole cerebrum is divided into two halves or hemispheres connected by a band of nerve fibers called the "corpus callosum."

To understand better what the brain looks like, form your hands into fists, so the thumbs are tucked in below. Move the fists together so that the outside of the thumb and pointing finger are toward you, and the pinkie is away. The fists are close to the size of the hemispheres of the brain. The tucked under thumbs point where the emotional brain would be. The outer layer is the cortex. The hindbrain or cerebellum, brain stem, etc. would be underneath your fists and away from you.

Rick Hanson, author of *Buddha's Brain*, writes, "Cortical tissues that are relatively recent, complex, conceptualizing, slow, motivationally diffuse sit atop subcortical and brain-stem structures that are ancient, simplistic, concrete, fast, and motivationally intense."[11] Ask your students what this means? What does he compare and contrast?

The brain has different "opponent processes." Hanson's quote refers to several oppositional processes, including cortical and subcortical, recent versus ancient, complex versus simple, slow versus fast. There is also a right and left hemisphere. The right side takes in more of the feeling or the whole picture, while the left more of the concepts, words. Ask these questions on opponent brain processing.

- What benefits, if any, do you gain from these opponent brain structures and ways of doing things? What detrimental effects might result from oppositional processes?
- What in your everyday life uses opponent processes? Students might ask if there is anything in life that does not depend on such processes.
- This is a form of built-in diversity. What is an advantage of diversity?

Diversity of viewpoints gives a more complex and thorough perspective. Without diversity, you might not learn enough to adapt. Perception relies on contrast. You see a black mark on a white board due to contrast. If the whole board were black, the markings would not show. Two eyes give more depth of vision than one. Two ears give us stereophonic hearing.

An Exercise in Imagination to Review and Anchor the Material

Use an exercise such as this if you studied a large amount of material in one day. If you study the brain through group presentations, you might ask the students to create review exercises. "Let's do a relaxing review. Sit up, close your eyes, and focus on your breath. With each in-breath, notice how your body responds. As you breathe out, notice what happens. Notice the relaxation and letting go. Simply relax in being here."

"Now, what did you learn today about the brain? Let's start with the lower, back area of your brain. Imagine putting your hand there, by the brain stem and cerebellum. What does that area of the brain do? Then move your hand up a few inches. What is that part of the cortex called? And what does it do?"

"The occipital lobe is the primary visual cortex. It searches for patterns, movement, shapes, location, and color. Then move your hand up further, to the top and just to the rear of the center of your head. Which lobe is there? What does it do? The parietal lobe is often called the 'where' area—it helps with touch, sense of physical self, and location in space. It also helps with visual information and cognitive skills like calculation."

"In the front part of the parietal there are the motor areas, which work with your senses and movement. Drop your hands to the sides of your head. Which cortex is on the sides? The temporal lobe is often called the 'what' area, concerned also with senses, particularly hearing, then vision. Inside from the temporal is also the area for taste. The temporal helps with language and memory."

"Now bring your imaginary hand to the front of the brain. Which cortex is there? What does it do? The frontal lobe includes the prefrontal cortex, which is responsible for what? Attention, planning, controlling emotion, interoception—doing what you're doing now, bringing things together. Other areas of the frontal are concerned with language and speech, imagining possible futures and the past, problem solving, etc. All this is yours, to use and remember. Now take a deep breath. Take in all that you studied. Then exhale. Let it sink in, and let your mind ready itself for whatever comes next."

"Open your eyes when you're ready, stretch, and have a good rest of the day."

LESSON NINE: THE EMOTION AREAS OF THE BRAIN AND HOW TO PAY ATTENTION

Reading for Discussion

- Daniel Goleman, *Emotional Intelligence: Why It Can Matter More Than IQ* (New York: Bantam Books, 1995), 13–24.
- Rick Hanson, *Buddha's Brain: The Practical Neuroscience of Happiness, Love, and Wisdom* (Oakland, CA: New Harbinger Publications, Inc., 2009) Extra Readings: 52–56, 97–108.

Frequently check on how well students do the practices. Hopefully, many do well and have taken a first step in mindfulness and use awareness to settle or calm themselves. A few might get stuck. Remind them that mindfulness is an experiment you conduct on yourself to determine what will calm you down and bring clarity to thinking. It is an opportunity to actively take charge of your life. If the practice for the day is not working, tell students to try some other practice. Or they can sit, relax and remember to be aware of what is happening now.

- The topics for today are the emotional areas of the brain, attention and mindfulness. Ask students: "Does emotion influence how you look at something? And if so, how?" This is the central question.
- "Name different ways you can be attentive or look at someone or something?" Think of the difference between a pitcher looking at a batter, a child looking at his mother, or a person looking spaced out.

Listen for student responses.

Mindfulness is the education of attention. There are actually three aspects of attention:

1. *What* you attend to.
2. *How* you attend. This is about the quality of attention.
3. The *intensity* of attention. High intensity with excitement and engagement or low intensity with disinterest and boredom.

The Practice

Emotion can define the way you attend to something. The exercise for the day will be very different than previous ones. It is based on a practice developed by psychologist, researcher, and author, Dr. Lawrence LeShan[12] and taught by him and Dr. Joyce Goodrich.[13] "How many of you have walked on a beach looking for treasures?"

How many hands shoot up?

You will need to gather small stones for this exercise. Polished stones work best. Small pieces of driftwood or shells are an alternative, or pine cones. Hold up a cloth bag filled with the stones. "This is a treasure bag. Today, each of you gets to pick a treasure from the bag. Pick one that stands out for you in some way."

Walk through the classroom and let students choose a stone.

"Put the stone on the table in front of you. Sit back from the table, at a comfortable distance so you can easily see the stone but not be right on top of it. Let your spine be straight but not rigid, and your head turned slightly down. Be comfortable. Then let your eyes close or be partly closed for a second, so you can stabilize your mind. Focus on breathing in, taking in awareness, oxygen. Then breathe out. Relax—let go of any thoughts or sensations except for being right here, right now."

"Now, partially and softly open your eyes, and gently put your attention on the stone. Let the attention be like what you give to someone you care for. Maybe think of a young pet you love. Or look at the stone as you would someone who needed you or loved you. Be active and alert, but instead of staring, focus gently. Bring as much of yourself as possible into this one act of simple looking, seeing, and caring. Look at the whole stone."

"Then look at different sections of it. Pick it up; study the shape, the colors, the patterns, texture, the feel, and the weight of the stone. Take in each detail. Let it live in your mind. Hold it up to the window, so you see the stone with the sky and hillside in the background. How is it with sunlight hitting it? Then put it down and close your eyes. Notice your breath and bring up the image of the stone. Turn the stone around in your mind so you see as much of it as you remember. Now, open your eyes and check on your memory. Does what you see, now, agree with your memory? And when you're ready, let go of the memory. Simply look with soft focus and care."

"Then, close your eyes, sit back and feel what it feels like to care. To care for something or someone other than you. To care, you also feel cared for. Just sit and appreciate being cared for. In a second, the bell will ring. When it does, calmly allow your attention to go to the whole room. Stretch, and get ready to re-join the class."

Ring the bell. Ask, "How was that? Was this a different sort of attention? How did it feel? How would you feel about giving back the stone?"

This can be a profound exercise for students. Allow them to share and process. It can be an exceptionally calming, even loving exercise. Anxious students might find it as one of the best practices for letting go of anxiety. For some students, the simple act of focusing intently on the stone can break them out of habitual patterns of sad or fearful emotion. For others, the stone is no longer merely a stone, but a valuable object. They might realize if they lose the value of simple, everyday things, they lose everything.

The discussion of the emotional brain can also provide an opportunity to challenge common ways people identify objects and think about the world. Try proposing the following questions:

* "How do your concepts, and ways of identifying and analyzing the world, influence what you perceive and how you feel?"
* "What occurs when you name something?"
* Think of the prefix *ex* as in the word "exist." It means "out," as in "exit" or get out. The rest of the word is from Latin *sistere* or the Indo-European *sta* meaning "to stand." Thus, when you say "this exists," you are making something "stand out" or appear separate.
* "Is your brain separate from your body?"
* "Is the emotional brain separate from the rest of the brain?[14] Is your nose separate from your face?"
* "The emotional areas of the brain have distinct functions. But does that mean emotions are dealt with only by the emotional brain?"
* "What does the emotional brain need? Does it need the rest of the brain? Does it need nutrients? Air? The world?"

Fear, worry, and anxiety arise from interpreting an aspect of the world as threatening. This gets worse if you interpret the sensory signal itself as threatening. An idea can be as threatening as a physical weapon but more insidious because it is more difficult to notice. Notice, breathe calmly, and then consider what you want to say or do. The next step is to connect experiential awareness with intellectual knowledge of how the brain constructs a sense of threat.

"What part of the brain is very involved in defending against a threat?" One central brain area is the amygdala.

If you want to use note-taking to help with memory, give students a note guide and draw on the blackboard or project on the whiteboard a diagram of the brain. Or send the student computers the guide and diagram. (See figure 2.2 for a diagram of the emotional brain.)

You could argue that the whole brain is involved in emotion. But the central emotion areas include the following: the thalamus (routing system), hippocampus, amygdala, and hypothalamus. Also included are the anterior cingulated cortex (which directs attention), orbito-frontal cortex (which Goleman calls an "instant social calculus"),[15] and the prefrontal cortex.

The amygdala is the "sentinel system"[16] which sets off the flight-fight response.[17] As Goleman describes, it scans "every situation, every perception,

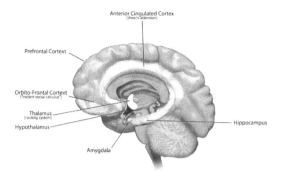

Figure 2.2   Sections of the Human Emotional Brain.

with but one question in mind, the most primitive: 'Is this something I hate? That could hurt me? Something to fear?'" If the answer is "yes," then it reacts instantaneously. It can even "hijack the brain" and get you to do things you might regret.[18] Try asking the following question(s):

- "What can this information on the amygdala reveal about what is given priority by our brain and sense system?" Anything that has to do with danger is given priority so that we react quickly to a possible threat.[19] "In what ways might it be important to know that your brain is primed to look for a threat?"
- "What happens to information which contradicts the danger signal?"
- "Why might it be important to understand that when you are frightened, your thinking can get distorted?"
- "Did you ever notice how frightening things could attract your attention? How easy is it to have negative thoughts about yourself or others?"
- "There are no direct connections from the amygdala to the verbal centers of the brain. Which is easier for you: To say why you are afraid? Or to say things driven by fear?"
- "You learn about yourself partly by watching how others respond to you. How might this affect your behavior? Did you ever hear about emotional contagion?"

Link what students learn about the brain with their experience of mindfulness. "What happens with the amygdala during meditation?" You might think it would shut down, but it remains active. The amygdala gives significance to signals the brain is receiving and provides a "feeling tone" to experience.[20] By controlling the feeling tone, it helps motivate how and what you do.[21] "Under meditative conditions. . .the activation of the amygdala confers emotional significance on the lack of incoming sensory information."[22] It recognizes that there is no danger and says you can open up. Imagine that. Offer the following questions to your students:

- "Imagine feeling open, free of danger in whatever classroom you are in. Would that change your associations with being in a classroom?"
- "When you look at a stone with a loving gaze, you feel affection. Is the affection in you or in the stone?"

Sometimes, people think mindfulness means to be detached. But what is attachment? If you project onto the stone the ability to make you feel good, bad or whatever, you become attached. The stone doesn't make you feel good. You do. Feeling good about a stone is feeling good. If the feeling for the stone interferes with your perception of whatever arises, then the attachment is harmful.[23] Mindfulness means you perceive whatever is there without holding on too tightly. You don't grasp too tightly, or push reality away, but something in between the two.

Mindfulness is a way to develop all your senses. Daniel Siegel conjectures that we have eight senses and not five. Sensing your "inner world" as when your heart clenches or your knees wobble is a sixth sense. This is called "interoception." The seventh is mental perception—comprehension of time, thoughts, images, and concepts. The eighth is reading others and the environment.

The first five senses are directed toward the external world, the sixth and seventh are more internal, and the eighth helps relate you to the whole of life.[24] These last three senses are what Siegel calls "mindsight."[25] To learn as much as you can from the first five senses, you need to develop the last three.

When you can mindfully let go, you enhance learning. The hippocampus stimulates neurogenesis—the production of new cells. You need new cells and new pathways for learning to take place. If you don't let go of stress and trauma, the hippocampus can shrink, and forming new memories and neurogenesis will be inhibited.

Students might wonder if this is what happens with PTSD (Post-Traumatic Stress Disorder) and if such loss is permanent. The research is not definitive but leans toward saying when you do mindfulness and stress reduction practices, brain cells in certain areas of the brain grow and function can be restored.

Before students leave for the day, ask them:

- "Name one fact that stands out for you?"
- The reading for the next day will be on what Daniel Goleman calls emotional hijackings. "Did you ever feel an emotion hijack your attention?" Have students raise their hands to express agreement or disagreement.

LESSON TEN: EMOTIONAL PATHWAYS
AND WHAT WE PAY ATTENTION TO

Readings for Discussion

- Daniel Goleman, *Emotional Intelligence*, 13–29.
- Richard Davidson, "Emotions from the Perspective of Western Behavioral Science," in *The Dalai Lama at MIT*, ed. Anne Harrington and Arthur Zajonc (Cambridge, MA: Harvard University Press, 2006), 141–150.

The previous lesson was on how you pay attention. Whether you focus with love or care, hate or anger. Whether you focus attention narrowly—like looking through a microscope—or broadly—as when looking up at the sky—this helps shape how you feel. The same with what you focus on and pick out from the vast world as an object of your attention. Understanding how emotions are formed and understanding attention overlap.

People of many cultures have used today's practice for over twenty-five hundred years.[26] It is one of the most important and common awareness practices and can eventually help you develop focused attention. You use counting as a way to focus and monitor your awareness of each breath. The sections of the prefrontal cortex, which are responsible for attention, are expanded and developed by this practice, as is your short-term memory.[27]

The Practice

Say to students, "Take a moment to settle yourself and turn to your breath. There are different ways to do this practice. Some people use it for their whole lives. What you do is silently and slowly count for yourself each breath, in and out. When you count, say the number to yourself throughout the breath. For example, breathe in, and say *oonnnnnnne*. Then exhale and say, *twwooooooo*."

"Keep attention on the count. Make the count focused but not tense. If a thought or sensation arises, recognize it and then return to the counting. Count each breath until you get to the number ten and then go back to one. Why? To remind yourself to maintain continuous awareness. If you keep going on to eleven, twenty, etc. you will get lost in the count. At home, use an alarm clock to signal when the practice is over. This way, you only need to pay attention to sitting and breathing, not time. Any questions?" Pause. "Enjoy."

During the practice, the class will most likely be extremely silent. Ring the bell as the signal to return attention to the class.

"How was that practice? Did you remember to count?"

Most students find this a simpler and calming way to practice mindfulness. Some will lose the count and get to twelve, thirteen, twenty. That's fine and common. You can joke about it. "At least you didn't get to one hundred."

Occasionally, a student finds the focus on the breath uncomfortable. They might be so habituated to spending mental energy distancing themselves from their own experience, especially of fear and discomfort, that when they let go of the distancing, they are in a new, clearer, mental space. They are aware of what before they hid away. Their discomfort can turn to anger and they will resist the practice. They need to understand what is happening and know experientially how to return attention to the counting.

A good topic for discussion is the illusion of multitasking. You can do more than one automatic, involuntary action at once, but the thinking mind can execute only one task and hold one object of focus in each moment.[28] Counting provides an alternative to fearful thoughts as an object of focus. Instead of reacting to difficult emotions or ideas with fear, you can learn to respond to them with gentleness, kindness, and openness, as you did with the stone.

When you hide away an aspect of yourself, you treat it as unforgiveable or wrong, and might think you are too weak to face it. You need to recognize that sometimes you are not ready, or the situation is not optimal, to think about a memory or a problem, and that is fine. But if you are simply aware of what arises—with curiosity and without getting caught up in it, as if it were merely a movie you were watching or you were hearing a good story—the feelings and thoughts diminish.

"Notice carefully how your mind works. You might have a sensation—then a feeling of aversion, of not liking it. Then you have the thought, 'This is anxiety.' Only then do you turn away. You get caught in a mean and nasty cycle; you feel aversion and then aversion to aversion." If students notice and analyze their anxiety in this way, their minds shift from being anxious to the practice of analysis.

"Your emotions and thoughts about them, even love and hate, don't arise fully developed in one step. They develop as a process. Even love at first sight arises as interest at first sight. Someone enters a room and right away you're watching him or her. That ever happen to you?" Listen for student responses and questions.

"Let's say you are walking through the woods. You hear a snap—a branch breaks. What is your response?" Listen for student responses.

"Do you stop, listen, and pay attention? Daniel Siegel calls it an 'initial orienting response.'[29] Your cognitive system is aroused but not yet engaged; you don't even know the sound as a twig."

"The next step is when memory kicks in. This process is important to recognize. It happens quickly. Memory brings the influence of the past over the present. Mindfulness can help you be aware of each step in the process. You can notice all of this as you appraise the moment." The appraisal includes:

a. Is this situation "good" or "bad?" You make it meaningful.
b. Energy is directed for action. Should you move toward or away?

c. Your state of mind is shifted in line with the appraised meaning. You label the event.

"You begin to form a representation or thought-image of a 'you' in the woods listening and a separate sound of the snap. According to Siegel, following the appraisal comes discrete emotions—fear, anger, sadness, joy. Emotions include nonverbal social signals—facial expression, posture, etc. You experience the meaning you have constructed ('there is a bear out there') and this influences the actions you ready yourself to take (run, duck, hide)."

"These signals tell others what is going on. For example, you hear the snap, your friends see your ears perk up and their ears perk up. You turn to run, and they prepare to run. This creates attunement. You feel 'felt' or acknowledged by recognizing that others are attuned to you. However, most of our emotional experiences are not of 'discrete' emotions but mixed emotional states."[30]

"If you notice the progression of responses in yourself you can place a 'gap' between sensation and thought, and between thought and action. What did the reading call an action in which you did not place these gaps, but instead reacted automatically, thoughtlessly, without the frontal cortex intervening?" This is what Daniel Goleman called a "hijacking."

Richie Davidson, a renowned neuroscientist, said that in the West we look at two axes of emotion: valence (whether the emotion is pleasant or unpleasant) and arousal (how strong it is).[31] Feeling tense might be high activation on the unpleasant side. Alert might be high activation on the pleasant side. Likewise, bored might be low activation. Buddhism adds another axis. Is the emotion afflictive—does it lead you to be agitated and to suffer? When you experience certain emotions, you feel you're suffering. Ask your students which emotions are like that for them.

There are also states of mind labeled virtuous—a mental state that "promotes well-being and freedom from inner compulsions which lead to suffering."[32] Hijackings easily lead to suffering. Virtuous states lead to happiness, flourishing, and a relaxed mind.

Then, get to the heart of the lesson. Ask students, "What are the two emotional pathways and how can they help explain emotional responses?" Listen to student answers. The "low road" is quick but sloppy. It is a direct pathway from the senses to the thalamus to the emotional centers of the brain. An emotional response is triggered before the "cortical centers have fully understood what is happening."[33] The low road involves the amygdala and the hypothalamus, the fight-flight-freeze system. The hypothalamus activates the pituitary gland, hormones, autonomic nervous system, physical behaviors—the four "fs" or feeding, fighting, fleeing, fornicating.

When the low road is used, you can respond in only 1/17th of a second. It enables fast but possibly afflictive results. It blocks out awareness of the initial orienting response as well as information that doesn't fit the developing emotion.

The low road ties you to the past. It is wired from incidents in your earlier life. The flame of a cooking stove burns you or a dog attacks you and from then on cook stoves and dogs set off a threat response. There is a saying in neuroscience: "What fires together wires together." Dog and bite happen together in time and wire together in your brain. The low road is called "sloppy" because there is "threat spread." Peripheral elements can be mentally associated with a threat that was not at all dangerous or even logically important. You might be attacked near a yellow house and forever after certain types of yellow houses set off a flicker of fear.

"Which parts of the brain are involved in the high road?"

The frontal lobe is the center of the high road. It is also significant that more parts of the brain are involved overall in the high road. The frontal, temporal and other sections get involved to reassess the original amygdala threat.

"When you see the yellow house, threat hormones are sent to your system, your body gets all hyped up and you get ready to flee. Then, when nothing awful occurs, you look more closely. Your frontal lobe questions the threat assessment. You, in the form of your frontal cortex, can step back from the situation, place a gap between sensation and thought, and between your thinking and behavior, and begin to shut down the low road. But hormones are slower than the electrical impulses in the nerves. There are some hormones left over in the system, so you still feel the jolt of fear for a while. Sound right? Ever feel that jitteriness in your stomach after a fright, even after you know there is nothing to fear?"

"When you're depressed and think no one will want to talk with you, or you get anxious about a presentation in class, this might be 'threat spread.' Your sense of one threat spreads to many threats—to your self-image, plans, relationships. How well you regulate emotion will depend on how you interpret the situation you are in. If you think you are capable of handling the situation, you do a better job than if you think you are not capable."[34]

To summarize and help pull the lesson together, suggest the following practice:

Practice to Assist Memory and Integration of Material

Tell students, "Right now, take a breath in, and out. Relax. If you want to close your eyes, feel free to do so. As you calmly breathe in, breathe in the class. Let images from the class, including words, ideas and feelings come to you. Allow yourself to absorb what we talked about. As you exhale, relax with it; let your mind settle. How did the class begin? What do you remember in the middle of the class? What happened near the end? What stood out for you? Let the material be there in your mind, ready when you need it. Then breathe in—and as you breathe out, open your eyes, feel awake, energized and ready to leave for the next class."

Ring the Tibetan bell.

NOTES

1. Christof Koch and Patricia Kuhl, "Decoding 'the Most Complex Object in the Universe,'" interview by Ira Flatow, *Talk of the Nation, NPR,* June 14, 2013, http://www.npr.org/2013/06/14/191614360/decoding-the-most-complex-object-in-the-universe.

2. Daniel J. Siegel, *Mindsight: The New Science of Personal Transformation* (New York: Bantam Books, 2010), 52.

3. Ibid., 51–52.

4. See the discussion in Jeremy Hayward, *Letters to Vanessa: On Love, Science, and Awareness in an Enchanted World* (Boston: Shambhala, 1997), 11–38.

5. George Lakoff and Mark Johnson, *Metaphors We Live By* (Chicago: University of Chicago Press, 1980), 3.

6. Rick Hanson, PhD, with Richard Mendius, MD, *Buddha's Brain: The Practical Neuroscience of Happiness, Love, and Wisdom* (Oakland, CA: New Harbinger Publications, 2009), 7.

7. Ramachandran, *Tell-Tale Brain,* 14.

8. Fritjof Capra, *The Tao of Physics* (New York: Bantam Books, 1976), 287.

9. Hanson, *Buddha's Brain,* 24.

10. Robert Ornstein and Richard F. Thompson, *The Amazing Brain* (Boston: Houghton Mifflin Company, 1984), 24.

11. Hanson, *Buddha's Brain,* 24.

12. Lawrence LeShan, *How to Meditate: The Acclaimed Guide to Self-Discovery* (New York: Bantam Books, 1975), 54–55.

13. "What is CRTP?" Consciousness Research and Training Project, accessed March 20, 2016, http://crtp.org/index.html.

14. Albert Low, *Genjokoan,* 23.

15. Daniel Goleman, *Social Intelligence: The New Science of Human Relationships* (New York: Bantam Books, 2006), 64, 171.

16. Goleman, *Emotional Intelligence,* 16.

17. Hanson, *Buddha's Brain,* 35.

18. Goleman, *Emotional Intelligence,* 17.

19. Hanson, *Buddha's Brain,* 40.

20. Ibid., 35–36.

21. Ibid., 101.

22. Dr. Shanida Nataraja, *The Blissful Brain: Neuroscience and Proof of the Power of Meditation* (London: Gaia Books, 2008), 88.

23. See Matthieu Ricard's discussion of this point in *The Dalai Lama at MIT,* Anne Harrington and Arthur Zajonc (Eds.) (Cambridge, MA: Harvard University Press, 2006), 173.

24. Siegel, *Mindsight*, 234.

25. Ibid., xiii.

26. B. Alan Wallace, *Mind in The Balance: Meditation in Science, Buddhism, and Christianity* (New York: Columbia University Press, 2009), 43–45.

27. James H. Austin, M. D., *Meditating Selflessly: Practical Neural Zen* (Cambridge, MA: MIT Press, 2011), 24–25.

28. Daniel Kahneman, *Thinking Fast and Slow* (New York: Farrar, Straus and Giroux, 2011), 22–23. Kahneman differentiates a fast, automatic, involuntary system from a slow, focused system requiring attention.

29. Siegel, *The Developing Mind*, 149.

30. Ibid., 149–153.

31. Dreyfus, in *The Dalai Lama at MIT*, 145.

32. Ibid., 145.

33. Goleman, *Emotional Intelligence*, 19.

34. Richard Davidson with Daniel Goleman, "Cultivating Emotional Skills," *Wired to Connect: Dialogues on Social Intelligence*, More Than Sound Productions, 2007.

Chapter 3

Emotion and the Quality of Your Mental State

Text Box 3.1   An Education that Relieves Suffering.

I taught a philosophy class, sometimes called Great Ideas, sometimes Questions. It was structured around the student's own questions about themselves and their lives, about death, love, mind, reality, truth, and ethics. The study of human emotion was central to the class. We often meditated in the class. One student commented, partly because of the meaningfulness of the discussions, partly because of the meditations, that the class was a great medication for relieving her depression.

The study of human emotion can yield profound results in how students function, not only throughout the school experience but also throughout life, and so is one of the most important subjects you can teach. You can teach about emotions using a variety of perspectives and disciplines.

1. Neuroscience of emotion—the science of the brain and the endocrine system.
2. Psychology—an intellectual understanding of why you have emotions, how they influence thinking, and the different components of emotion.
3. Mindfulness of emotion—learn from emotions and let them go when you need to; develop awareness of emotional triggers, sensations, facial expressions, thoughts, habits, and inclinations to act.
4. Language of emotion—emotional literacy to pinpoint and speak about what is going on inside yourself.

LESSON ELEVEN: THE LANGUAGE
AND STUDY OF EMOTION

Emotional literacy not only helps you live your emotions in a healthier manner, but also helps you learn more. You become more aware of how you process new information and you interact more empathically with other students. By interacting with others in a more empathic and aware manner, you slow the rush for answers or closure and are able to relate more to the material studied.

Students in a high-school class were asked to define wisdom. They rebelled against the word and denied there is such a thing. It's something that sounded good and they wished it was real, but they didn't think it existed except as an arena for judging themselves negatively. Yet, they knew wisdom intuitively when they encountered it. Maybe wisdom is like love, a word so wrapped in competing concepts and experiences that clarity seems impossible. If wisdom includes knowing yourself and how to act without harming others in the world, emotional awareness is a key to wisdom.

The Practice

Start the class by asking if students have any questions about breath counting practice. Wait for questions.

"After practicing breath counting for a few months, your thinking will get more flexible and it will be easier to let go of disturbing thoughts. Let's do the practice, now, but with a slight alteration." If you teach only one form of breath counting, teach it this way.

"Today, gently be aware of each inhalation, and count only with the exhalation. After you exhale, your body wants to inhale. Allow yourself to breathe in. Let it be easy and natural. Then focus on the exhalation and say a number, starting with *one* for the first exhalation. Count *oonnnnnee* all through the breath. Then say *twwooooo* with the next exhalation, and so on. Count only up to ten."

"Instead of going to eleven, go back to one. As you exhale and silently utter each number to yourself, use that utterance to pull your attention to the moment of the breath. Do it as an exercise that you love. The word 'remember' can mean to come back home, to put your mind back in your body. Now, let's do the practice of counting ourselves back into our own awareness. The bell will ring after two minutes."

Ring the bell after two minutes. Students will calmly return their attention to the classroom.

"How was that practice?"

Students, as with any exercise, get better with practice at remembering to count and to refocus their attention when they drift. Some will have to learn how to coordinate the count with the breath, so the two don't conflict or they don't unconsciously slow it down or speed it up.

"Each person is different. Use whichever mindfulness practices you find most helpful and natural. The awareness of the breath makes you more aware of unconscious patterns, thus enabling you to let go of them."

The philosopher, Zen teacher and author David Loy said that when you start practicing this, you eventually notice that there is you counting, you breathing, and a third "person" who introduces other thoughts or images or sensations.[1] Eventually, the thoughts slow down and disappear. You focus only on breathing and counting. It becomes natural. You are simply present. You barely know there is a you. It is pure process, pure seeing or hearing. "You" are not breathing. Rather, you are "being breathed."[2] Underlying all your conscious events is this presence. Even when you are focused on some object, this essential awareness is there. But you don't usually notice it. Without it, the mind would be too "full" to notice anything.

Ask students to take out their journals and draw a line down the middle of a page to create two columns. Tell students to complete the assignment as follows:

- In one column, record the emotions you frequently experience. In the second column, write down a list of emotions you experience rarely.
- If students ask what you mean by frequently, suggest the emotions they have felt recently, or ones that are very familiar to them.
- If they ask you for a definition of emotion, tell them to use their own definition for now.
- "Who would like to share two or three emotions they frequently experience?"

The chart below shows the emotions listed by students in one class and a number indicating how many of them mentioned each one. (See table 3.1) Anger, frustration, stress, anxiety, love, and affection are the most frequently experienced. Sadness, guilt, hatred, fear, and anger were the ones listed as least experienced. There are inconsistencies in student responses, especially with fear. Fear will often appear as "frequently experienced" on student's actual lists and journals but only infrequently mentioned in class.

Students will often be so engaged and boisterous that you will get through only the first column of emotions—those they frequently experience. In that case, do the second column on the following day. You will hardly have to say anything during the class aside from calling on students to share. You can record words on the board and occasionally ask if _____ is an emotion and why. Even better, let a student do the recording.

By giving so much of the class over to the students, you empower and give them the opportunity to monitor themselves. In one class, in the middle of the discussion, a student looked over the class and made a critical statement. "Look at yourselves. You're all over the place." If necessary, ask students to notice their own breathing and carefully listen to each other. The students

Table 3.1   Emotions Experienced Frequently and Infrequently

Emotions Frequently Experienced	Emotions Infrequently Experienced
4 - Stress	2 - Sadness
4 - Anger/frustration	2 - Deep Anger
4 - Love, Affection	2 - Guilt
4 - Anxiety	2 - Hatred
3 - Excitement	2 - Fear
3 - Happiness	Jealousy
3 - Joy	True Love
2 - Jealousy	Resentment
2 - Confusion	Confidence
2 - Apathy	Security
Exasperation	Self-Pride
Shame/embarrassment	Paranoia
Guilt	Anxiety
Fear	Disappointment
Worry	Contentment
Appreciation	Frustration
Loneliness	Calm, Chill
Sadness	Closure
Depression	
Irritation	
Calm	
Wonder	
Trapped	
Empty	
Removed	
Curiosity	
Humor	
Respect/admiration	

have a vast universe of inner experience but know how to consciously deal with, and allow, only a small portion of that universe, especially in a school context.

Suddenly, in this lesson, the universe of experience and language will be expanded. It is wild and greatly meaningful for students to see and hear what other students feel. They step out of isolation and separation, outside of their normal ideas about themselves and the world.

At the end, ask your students what stood out for them from the lesson.

LESSON TWELVE: WHAT IS EMOTION?

Reading for Discussion

- Daniel Goleman, *Emotional Intelligence: Why It Can Matter More Than IQ* (New York: Bantam Books, 1995), 3–14.

Sometimes, school will be unpredictably noisy and jumpy, as with the first snow of the year, a warm day in winter, or if something disturbing happens to a student in the class. You can adapt the mindfulness practice to fit the mood of the day. And when students understand their own emotional responses, they can more easily adapt to whatever situation they encounter.

One thing to teach students is how to face, without panic, not only an uncomfortable thought but an unexpected, even a disturbing, situation. Mindfulness can save lives. When emotions light up like the explosions they witness, you need to be strong and clear-headed. You have to be mindful of what you feel in order to act appropriately with it.

Linda Lantieri, educator and founding member of Collaborative for Academic, Social, and Emotional Learning (CASEL), talked about how teachers in a school near Ground Zero in Manhattan on September 11, 2001, were able to lead five thousand elementary school students to escape the school and the area quickly, despite debris falling all around them, with no loss of life. This took "inner preparedness."[3]

Tell students, "Sometimes, the unexpected occurs and you feel your intentions frustrated. But an obstruction can become a great teaching. Did you ever, at first, think something was the worst thing in the world, and then, later, you love it?" Listen to student responses.

"G. K. Chesterton, a novelist, said: 'An adventure is only an inconvenience rightly understood.' How about we practice turning a small obstruction into a mini-adventure?"

The Practice

Direct students to take a gentle breath in and then let it go. "Feel the inhalation. Feel what your body does as you breathe in. Then breathe out, and feel that, too. Listen to the breath as you breathe in. Then as you breathe out, listen to that. There's nothing else you have to do right now. If you hear anything else, that's fine. It's just a sound or a thought. A thought can be like a passing sound, a wind created by mind. Just listen to it come up and listen to it go. A sound or thought is just there for you to notice."

"Listen to the quality of it. Become a connoisseur of sound. Maybe you hear a sound in the hall—it's just a sound. Maybe you hear a bird call; listen to it as if the sound of birds was the sound of wherever you felt most at home. Listen to high notes, or low notes. Or pitch. Even hall noise is its own form of music, the music of the school."

"In between the notes of this natural music, there is silence. Hear this silence between the notes. Without the silence, there is no music. Notice how the silence feels. Awareness has the possibility of noticing and letting go of anything. The calmness of silence can spread through everything you hear, everything you are aware of. Of what are you aware? Notice it. Then notice that you are aware. That's what your consciousness is—awareness. Sit, now, in that silent awareness. Sit in listening itself. Settle into that quality of attention that is there for whatever arises. Enjoy it."

After a few seconds, ring the bowl.

Then ask students to respond to the following questions by writing in their journals:

1. What came up for you in the mindfulness practice?
2. What questions do we need to cover about emotion?

Collate student responses and follow-up with these student questions:

- "What is emotion?"
- "How come our emotions can sometimes get us to do such wrong things?"
- "What is a 'healthy' love?"
- "How much of emotion is genetic and how much environmental?"
- "Can you live without emotion?"
- "Why have emotions?"
- "What happens in us when we have an emotion?"
- "What is the difference between a mood and an emotion?"
  Students often ask to study specific emotions like anger, fear, love, happiness or satisfaction, and anxiety. Incorporate student questions into your class whenever and however you can.
- "What is an emotion? This is more complicated than you might think. Everyone has feelings, sensations and thoughts. Which of your experiences do you call emotion?"
- "I think there are times when people are not sure what they feel. Were you ever unsure what you felt? If emotions are so obvious, how can you be unsure about them?"

Western psychology provides several theories about what emotions are. For example, are emotions what get us to act? Or are emotions our understanding of our bodily response to actions we have already taken? Is fear, for example, a response to a situation, which gets us to act? Or is the fear how we interpret our own response? William James, for example, said, "We don't see a bear and then experience fear and then run. Instead, we see the bear, start running and feel our heart beating, and then feel fear."[4] Many people think of emotion as a feeling, or sensation. "Are emotions only sensations? Do sensations come with thoughts and stories attached?" Let the questions sit for a moment.

Tell students, "We imagine emotions are clear and distinct; they can certainly hit us powerfully, but their power can hide their nature. Emotion can feel like it is what makes you *you.*" Emotions are powerful and, thus, easy to identify with. Students might feel emotion is the most honest and real part of them. A life without emotion can seem a horrifying prospect. "When an emotion goes away, do you disappear? If not, then are they really *you?*"

"'In traditional Indian and Tibetan Buddhist texts there does not seem to be any word which comes even close to our concept of emotion.'[5] Emotions are thought of as mental states, similar to states like clarity and compassion. Emotions might be more elusive then we think, and as much a personal or cultural construction as biological. What does Daniel Goleman say about what an emotion is in the reading?"

The root of "emotion" is "motere," *to move.*[6] Emotions get us to move. An emotion is "a feeling and its distinctive thoughts, psychological and biological states, and range of propensities to act." They don't always get us to act, but instead create a readiness and energy to act.[7] Anger enables us to attack quickly, disgust to turn away, joy to embrace.

Ask students, "Do we need these quick reactions as much as we did thousands of years ago?" Invite the students to dig deeper. "Did we live in cities or villages thirty or one hundred thousand years ago?"

"If emotions serve a survival function, how can they go so wrong sometimes?" How often do you walk down the street and encounter a saber-toothed tiger? Or a cave bear? Over 40,000 years ago there were cave bears that were nine feet tall. Humans evolved to be able to react quickly to a life-death situation, then relax, and spend most of the time hanging out. Yet, even though most people live today in towns and cities, our bodies and brains are relatively the same as they were thirty or a hundred thousand years ago.

"Today, hopefully, where do you discover most of your life-death situations?" (Emphasize *hopefully.*) Students might respond with answers that include war, the streets of a city, movies, television, or video games.

"When you watch the screen and a monster comes after you, you respond as if you were actually threatened. Or, when someone disrespects you, your body responds to the threat to your self-image as if it was a threat to your life. How many of you repeat negative comments people say about you over and over?" Listen for student responses.

"That's stress. When you do that, you keep the emotion going. You re-stimulate the fear. Emotions are meant to be short lived. But if you are not aware of what emotions are and what you feel, you might keep them going and stress yourself."

"Besides quick responses, what other purposes do emotions serve?" Listen for the wide range of student responses. *They make life worth living. They express what matters to us. They connect us so we can work together.*

Joseph Chilton Pearce and others call Paul MacLean's emotional brain the "relational brain."[8] Emotions relate us to others, and to our environment, and can guide or interfere with thought. An important part of the relational brain is the insula, located in the back of the frontal lobe. It helps ready us to act. Compassion practices activate the insula. Someone asked how people could ignore screams for help. Anger can turn you away from perceiving another person's needs. If the insula has been activated, a person will respond more readily to end another person's suffering and see the situation more clearly.

To clarify how you can ignore or totally misperceive what is around you, ask: "When you feel depressed, is it easy to imagine enjoying yourself?" Listen to student responses.

Depression is not only a depressed mood but a depressed ability to take in new information. When depressed, you can experience what psychologists call a refractory period during which "we cannot reconsider, we cannot perceive anything that is inconsistent with the emotion we are feeling."[9] This can happen with other emotions like hate, disgust, and fear, which are uncomfortable. They tell you to turn away from an aspect of the world. It is in the nature of such emotions to keep awareness out.[10] When you are open-minded and engaged, you turn toward the world. You experience joy, wonder, love, and compassion. Feeling good is likely to help you embrace and integrate what you are learning.

In this way emotions give a meaning to events. Did you ever notice how, after having an enjoyable time with someone special, maybe listening to a song by Santana, and from then on whenever you hear that song or are in that location you feel good and regret ever leaving that location?

The researcher, Douglas Watt, said: "Emotion binds together virtually every type of information the brain can encode. . . .It is part of the glue that holds the whole system together."[11] "When integration is enhanced, our state of well-being is improved," elaborates Daniel Siegel. We feel close to others, healthy. "In contrast, if we've had an emotionally disturbing experience" integration is disturbed; we might experience chaos or rigidity. Some emotions might limit integration, like anxiety and hatred, while others enhance it.[12] Maybe emotion is like music. It directs your attention by giving an emotional tone to a moment.

Emotion can wrap you into itself. Paul Ekman says emotion can be triggered quickly through an almost automatic interpretation you give to a situation. It is this interpretation or appraisal and response to an initial stimulus that is most important. You are not always aware of what's driving you and thus have trouble changing the emotion.[13]

It might seem that if emotions evolved to help us survive, how then can we dare to alter or change them? Does genetics argue that people are born angry, depressed, manipulative, or loving? Are the only choices nature or nurture? Can't one of the choices be both? What does neuroplasticity say about genetic inheritance? Ekman outlines four dimensions of possibly inherited emotional patterns or profiles.[14] The rest is nurture. There are a few inherited patterns or triggers of what sets off a person. Then there is the:

1. amplitude or strength of an emotion, how strongly we get emotional.
2. onset speed or how fast emotions arise in us.
3. duration.
4. recovery or how quickly the emotion dissipates.

"What are the components or building blocks of emotion?" The following analysis is based on what was already discussed about modern Western approaches[15] as well as Buddhist[16] teachings.

Emotions consist of feelings, sensations, thoughts, and the appraisal you make or story you tell yourself about a trigger or situation, and actions you consider taking. Each emotion has a use or a possible purpose in life, but you can lose sight of this purpose.

Feelings—These include awakening attention, then a sense of something being pleasant, unpleasant, or neutral, which leads to attraction, aversion, or disinterest.

Sensations—Your body undergoes physiological changes (such as increased heart rate, sweating, blood flow to certain areas) when you are emotional, and you can sense many of these changes. They signal (with facial expressions, tone of voice, posture, etc.) to yourself and others what you're going through. Learning to notice the sensations, and how others respond to your signals, increases your ability to learn from or let go of emotion. Sensations can be broken down into:

• Location (where you "feel" it, such as knees for fear)
• Quality (e.g., embarrassment might feel hot, fear might seem cold, worry might itch)
• Intensity

Thoughts—You hold beliefs about the world or tell yourself a story about a person who wronged you or a situation that is glorious. This inner dialogue can be like a script you repeat or an imaginative experiment you conduct in your mind. You might create images in your mind and feel judgmental of yourself or another person.

Actions—You consider actions to take which fit your beliefs, the story you tell and feelings you have.

Students often ask about moods. "What is a mood? How is it different from emotion?" Maybe you feel something and label it as a mood but find defining it difficult. Emotions are generally short lived, but moods can last a long time. They tend to persist and are usually more diffuse or subtle.[17] Daniel Goleman says that moods "tend to reflect that person's overall sense of well-being."[18]

Emotions relate you to time. Fear relates you to the future, guilt to the past. A mood does something similar. It helps create the background of your day, or background to a certain type of situation. Stories and cultural myths give you the overall context in which you live. Maybe a mood establishes a context for your experience.

Ask for volunteers to sum up what emotions are.

"Tomorrow, we will hopefully answer one of life's deepest concerns: How can you diminish your own suffering and that of others?"

LESSON THIRTEEN: A PHILOSOPHICAL AND BUDDHIST INQUIRY INTO SUFFERING

Readings for Discussion

• Steve Hagen, *Buddhism Plain and Simple* (New York, Broadway Books, 1997), 1–24.
• David Loy, *Money, Sex, War, Karma* (Boston, Wisdom Publications, Inc., 2008), 15–23.

One year, in a literature class, on the day after a class member was involved in an automobile accident, the scheduled lesson was on suffering. Because of the accident and wanting to acknowledge and process feelings, emotional healing became the practice for the day.

Talking about any fear and worry that we all share helps students learn that pain and suffering are as normal as joy and love. Often people add an extra layer to pain. They believe loss, difficulties, and mistakes are abnormal and indicate something wrong in you or in your character. Pain is awful enough. Why add this extra layer of suffering?

Some students may be concerned that if they talk about suffering they will become more depressed. Assure them you won't forget joy and pleasure.

"Today we will center on the psychology of suffering. It might sound depressing, especially today. But, if we understand what is hidden within suffering, will we be better equipped to prevent or diminish it? By understanding suffering we can better understand our previous discussion of emotions and what makes them hurtful. And then joy and pleasure will be more accessible to us. But first, what if we do a healing meditation?" Listen for student responses.

The Practice

Direct students to take a moment to settle themselves on their chair and to get comfortable. "Close your eyes partly or fully. And as you breathe in, just go with it. Allow yourself to feel the air filling you, expanding with energy and life. What does it feel like to breathe in? And out? As you breathe out, feel yourself relax, let go, settle down. Just go with this natural rhythm and ease into it."

"When you're ready, allow yourself to think of a time that X was laughing, or doing something joyful and expansive. Just watch him. What was his laugh like at that moment? How did he gesture? What was he doing that led to his laughter? Now think of a time when you had a positive or meaningful interaction with him. What was the situation? What did you do or talk about? If you never had such a sharing with him, imagine doing so. Imagine talking with him, or walking around campus or eating lunch with him."

"Now imagine a ball of healing light above your head, maybe white, or blue. This ball is filled with good health, energy, laughter. Fill this light with all the warmth and positive images that come to mind. If it is difficult to imagine this ball of light, picture the sun on a nice day and feel the way the sun can be so welcoming and healing. Then, imagine this light going out from you, from your head or heart, to his. Imagine it going from his head to his shoulders and down to his feet, filling him with light. Imagine how he might respond to this light and warmth."

"Now imagine the light coming back to you, from him to you. Feel or picture the light coming from him to you. And then the whole pathway, from your mind to his and back again. Imagine one brilliant light encompassing both of you. How does it feel to be filled by light, joy, healing? Sit for a moment with a sense of a healing light or energy filling you both."

Let the singing bowl sing.

After the practice, ask students: "Take a few minutes to record in your journal what you think suffering is. Make a list of situations in which you might suffer mentally or emotionally." (Everyone, including the teacher, should write in their journal.)

"How do you feel now?"

Listen to student responses. This practice can be emotional for students. Students often report that the experience is extremely moving and almost brought them to tears. They are thankful for the opportunity to do this together in school. "Then ask:

"What situations did you put on your list?" Record on the chalkboard or white board the students' responses. The list will grow long quickly. The loss of a friend—through an argument, moving away, even death. Fighting with a parent. Feeling oppressed and unfulfilled. Inability to make a loved one happy. War. Feeling poor. Loneliness. Guilt."

More entries might be chalked onto the board on the front wall. Uncertainty. Regret. Not expressing an emotion. An unresolvable conflict.

A question without an answer. The struggle to deal with something unpleasant or confusing. *"Wasting my life." "Getting old." "Or not being able to live long enough to get old."*

Then, focus the students on reflecting on and analyzing their responses.

- "What do these all share?" What do you hear in these statements, not just content, but feeling? Students suggest denial—denial of who they are as a person. Anger.
- "Does all suffering include a sense of loss?"
- *"You can't lose what you never had,"* said one student. *"I never had most of the things I yearn for."*
- "Philosopher David Loy used the word 'lack' to express the analysis and feeling of suffering. Does the word work for you?"
- *"There is something here about feeling inadequate, or like something is missing, in me,"* replied one student.

A student response may introduce a crucial point of The First Noble Truth in Buddhism: the presence in life of what the Buddha calls *Dukkha*. This word is from Pali, the language spoken by the Buddha. It is often translated as suffering, although that is not the best definition. Steve Hagen, in the assigned reading, says Dukkha means to feel off, or dissatisfied. Think of a wheel out of kilter; like a bicycle wheel out of true round. Imagine what it would be like to ride such a bike. Use Buddhist teachings as a possibly useful perspective to examine and question and not as material to merely accept.

"Lack is one way to describe the feeling of suffering, but it's not the cause. What might be a cause of suffering?"

Wait a moment in silence for the students to think about suffering as a symptom and what might be the source. They might want to jump to attributing the cause of suffering to relationships and external factors before fully understanding the experience.

"In Buddhism, the cause of suffering is spelled out in the Second Noble Truth. In Pali, the word used is *Tanha* which means *thirst* and selfish desire."

"Do attachments cause suffering?" The question applies their initial grasp of suffering as a sense of lack to their understanding of the pain that arises in emotional attachments. Ask students what attachment means to them and record responses.

Often, a fear of attachment will be revealed. Students say any attachment, any caring or love, is threatened by loss and suffering, yet they deeply desire bonds of affection and affirmation. Love and fear of loss can go together, but it's painful to think about.

It is important to understand that: "Impermanence is part of any relationship but is not, by itself, the cause of suffering."

The reading in *Buddhism Plain and Simple* includes the story of the Buddha who said he could not help a man with his 84th problem, the problem of wanting to not have problems. Ask students what the story means to them.

"What happens when you go into a store and see a pair of running shoes that you are dying to have?" Try to ground the concept of lack in their experience. "Or you see an iPad or a Droid and have images of who you would be if only you had that gadget. Or maybe you're about to get your driver's license or you have a license but you want to buy your own car. You have this image of a future you. It is exciting. But let's say you don't get the shoes or the gadget or the car—what a bummer. What happens?" Listen for student responses.

"Or, you get what you want and you are so happy. But two days or a week later, you develop this idea or feeling of lacking something else. And you go through the same dance of desire and deficiency."

The Third Noble Truth in Buddhism is that suffering can cease. The Fourth offers an Eight-Fold Path to end suffering. It teaches awareness and analysis of one's own experiences and emotions so suffering can be decreased or ended. This is a lot for students to process. It is also not the whole answer. Students will readily discern that something as complex as suffering cannot be put into too tidy a bundle.

"For tomorrow, there's a reading in Goleman, called 'Passion's Slaves.' Anyone know who Goleman quotes?" Some students might recognize the quote from Shakespeare, *Hamlet*, "Give me that man/That is not passion's slave, and I will wear him/In my heart's core"[19]

LESSON FOURTEEN: WHAT IS ANGER?

Reading for Discussion

• Daniel Goleman, *Emotional Intelligence*, 59–65.

To increase engagement and make the learning more personal, for homework ask students to describe a time they felt anger. Include all the components: What triggered the emotion, the physical sensations, thoughts, and actions you wanted to take in response? Would you respond the same way that you did if it happened to you again? If you had more insight at the time, what could you have done differently? Such mental reenactment is often helpful.

The Practice

Tell the class, "It's time to check in with yourself. How about closing your eyes, and relaxing into your breath. Place your attention on noticing or sensing whatever arises in your mind and body. What is the feel of your feet on the floor? What is the sense of your hands in your lap." Pause for a moment.

"What other sensations do you notice? What is the quality of the sensation? Is there tension or tightness? Resistance? Or openness, calmness? Notice what happens when you become aware of a feeling or sensation. Notice how it changes."

"Do you hear any thoughts arising? Notice the thoughts and how they arise—and then how they dissipate."

"Now, mentally step back. Picture someone who is a bit angry, as if you are watching him or her on a movie screen or at a distance. What does he or she do? What kind of gestures does he or she use? What do you imagine he or she is feeling? Where does he or she feel it? What might have led this person to do what she or he did?"

"Then imagine: 'The person I am angry at—she once helped me and was kind to me.' Imagine him or her being kind. How does that change things?"

"Now imagine forgiveness; imagine the once angry person forgiving the person he or she was angry at.[20] What does forgiveness look like? Think about what actions show it or words express it. Imagine the feeling of forgiving someone." Pause for a few seconds and then add, "What does it feel like to be forgiven? Sit for a moment with the feeling of being forgiven."

After the practice, ask students to write in their journals and describe what came up for them about forgiveness. After a minute or so, give out a sheet with an outline of a human body and ask students to circle the places where they feel anger.

Then ask them to form triads, groups of three, and share with the other students "What triggers anger?" After about 6 minutes, ask the whole class:

- "Anyone want to share what came up for you in the visualization, or what changed in you by forgiving the other person?"
- It's not easy to forgive. For many, it will feel impossible or artificial. Yet, when you forgive someone, or yourself, a great burden is lifted. It is powerful. Students might express a feeling of being hugged. They might feel at the point of tears.
- "What happened to the anger when you thought of the other person's viewpoint?"

Physical expression of emotion is obviously important in communication. One source[21] quoted a study saying that words are only seven percent of communication. Fifty-five percent of the emotional message is expressed through the face, posture and gesture and thirty-eight percent through tone of voice. So, what is the physical face of anger?

- "Where do you feel anger?"

Students often mention their hands and feet, others the stomach or the mouth.

- "When you are angry, what actions do you want to take?"
- "Does anger feel good?"

Some will feel anger is powerful, others that it hurts and will be frightened by it.

"Can you show what an angry face looks like?"

This can excite the class. Students show eyebrows down, lips tight, chin forward.[22]

"What is the quality of the sensations of anger?"

Students might mention:

Like jumping out of your skin.
Tense—I get tense, like a tightly strung wire.
I want to scream.
It's like a burning sensation, but I don't want anyone to see it.
I get jumpy, shaky. I can't be still. My hands want to move around.
I feel squashed, like someone or something is sitting on my chest.

- "Can anyone share what your group discovered about the triggers for anger?"

Students might mention:

When someone says something to hurt or attack us, or make us feel small.
When we feel ignored or suppressed.
Or someone verbally or physically attacks someone or something we like.
If we feel our goal is blocked or that we can't get what we want.
If someone can't understand something obvious, like how important is the quality of the air we breathe.

- "Every emotion developed for a purpose, although the reason for the emotion might not be as appropriate in our world as it was in the past. What is the use of anger?"

Students might respond:

It gets us ready to defend ourselves.
It is full of energy. I can feel very alive when I'm angry.

Can anger sometimes serve a positive purpose? The psychological researcher, Richard Davidson, says yes. Anger can possibly help you overcome an obstacle.[23] It can get you to pay attention, wake up to something. The Dalai Lama once said a righteous anger over someone being hurt, for example, can be helpful.[24] If anger is not followed by aggression, blame, shame, and hurt but is met with awareness and compassion, then it can be a message to stop what you're doing and decrease suffering. But if it becomes "do that and I'll hit you" or you turn anger against yourself, then it is afflictive.

"Let's look a little more at the psychology of anger. How many of you drive?" Listen for student responses.

"Ever have a person cut you off, speed by you and almost knock you off a road? What would go on in your mind if you were cut off like that? What thoughts might you have?"

Question students in order to uncover images and possibly an underlying story they tell themselves. Anger is built out of thoughts like: "How dare he do that to me!" You feel put down. It's not just being endangered; you imagine the person intended to slight you. A sense of righteousness follows. You feel you were right, he was wrong, and you are attached to that viewpoint. You tell yourself a story of an injustice that has been committed.

"Yet, imagine you follow the driver and he or she leads you to a hospital. What might you then feel?" This changes everything. You tell yourself a very different story. You might feel sheepish or embarrassed by your anger. You think up stories to explain why the driver is at the hospital.

Notice the image you create of yourself and the other person. Your image of yourself as the wronged person and the other as the doer-of-wrong need each other. It is like being on a teeter-totter. In order for you to go up, your partner must go down. It is not just the actual or "external" stimuli that triggers an emotion but the "internal" context, your memories, culture, the way you create a story out of the event. In effect, it is a whole situation that triggers emotion.

To get students to broaden their perspective on their emotions, ask: "Can stress, or a hurtful incident early in the day, make you more prone to anger later on?"

"How about when someone insults you. And later in the day, you enter a new situation, you hear someone giggling, and what do you think or imagine?" Students will often share interesting responses.

Then: "What are different kinds or intensities of anger?"

Draw on the blackboard a line from left to right. Label the left "low intensity" and the right "high intensity" and record, in the appropriate location, where students think the emotion fits. Irritation, sulking, and annoyed might fit on the left, and rage, wrath, and seething on the right.[25]

"Whom do you get most angry at? People you care about or those you don't?" This question could also be asked about *what* gets you most angry.

"When we talk about love we will study why we usually get most angry at those who are closest to us. When we love, we care. Care, love primes us to respond even to emotions that seem opposite them. This is another lesson on emotion: it can move us toward something by pushing us away from something else."

"Tomorrow we will diagram all this in terms of the components of anger and talk about how to intervene in it."

LESSON FIFTEEN: SHOULD I OR SHOULDN'T I? ANGER AND KINDNESS

Reading for Discussion

• Reread Daniel Goleman, *Emotional Intelligence*, 56–77.

To learn how to intervene in an emotion, students need to realize that their whole lives can be a mindfulness practice. Establish the atmosphere that each moment in class, especially each discussion, is an opportunity to learn, about yourself, and from others. One way to do this is to occasionally stop the class and ask: "What were you thinking about or feeling? Was there any resistance to hearing what someone else said?" And occasionally, especially in discussing a topic like anger, ask the students to repeat what they heard a student say before responding to it.

You can use improvisational theater exercises to help students learn to pay attention to another person's body messages. Mirroring is one such exercise. Ask two people to stand and face each other, hands up and open, slightly in front, facing the hands of their partner. Imagine that the surface of the mirror is halfway between you. One person leads, the other mirrors. Move slowly, never break eye contact or break the mirror. An example of breaking the mirror would be if the leader's right hand goes outward, toward her partner and past the partner's left hand.

Collect homework descriptions of an example of experiencing anger. Later on, give students a chance to share their stories. Then say to students, "Today, we will talk about anger, freedom, and kindness. I don't know about you, but I like when people treat me kindly. How about just for today we start our practice with a little kindness?"

The Practice

Direct students to take a second to let their bodies settle down. Say, "As you close your eyes or soften the focus of your gaze, breathe in and hold it; then breathe out and let it go. Gently allow yourself to center on just being here. As you breathe in, focus your mind on the act of breathing in. As you breathe out, let all other thoughts, feelings just dissolve away so you can relax with being aware, here, now."

"Imagine kindness. Picture or feel an act of kindness, either one you witnessed, or one you read about or imagined. What was the act of kindness? Who was the person acting kindly? What did the kind person do? What words or gestures were used?" Pause for a few seconds. "When you hear the word *kindness* what other words also pop into your mind?"

"How does it feel to be kind? How does it feel when someone is kind to you? Just rest for a second in the feeling of being kind and being treated with kindness."

Ring the singing bowl.

The class will take a moment to emerge from silence. When the students look up, then ask, "Was kindness easy to imagine?" Allow a sharing of responses. Students frequently ask:

- *Why does kindness feel so rare? Shouldn't it feel common?*
- *Maybe we don't feel that we should do it, that it is as important as completing our assignments or jobs.*
- *Is kindness something you can practice?*
- Reply: "Yes—We just did it."
- *Why be kind, besides the fact that it feels good?*
- Responses include: *"It makes relating to others easier." "It improves the whole group." "I feel more awake when I'm kind." "Kindness makes me feel more complete; I think I only recently realized that. Just smiling at someone can change my mood." "Did you ever notice how you respond when someone smiles at you? Imagine smiling at your heart or your stomach or your eyes."*
- *How does kindness relate to anger?*
  Listen to student responses. Anger can bring the impulse to attack, even hurt; kindness to soothe, to really see, care.

Remind students, "We talked about the first priority of the brain is protection, so it is easier to feel angry than kind. The frontal lobe has to turn off emotions like anger in order for you to feel happiness or joy. If you are often greedy or angry, you make greed or anger easier to feel. But if you practice being kind, then joy, happiness, calm develop readily."

This can raise the question in students: *"Does this mean anger is more truly me?"*

Remind students about the stage of emotion called the "orienting response." "To orient yourself, you first need awareness. Matthieu Ricard, an author, Buddhist monk, with a degree in biology, talks about the first impulse of anger, or any emotion, is 'basic awareness. . .which is like a mirror that is not intrinsically tainted with negativity or obscuration.'[26] The hostility, or the desire for revenge and all those afflictive qualities of anger, come after the attention is there, when all the thoughts and appraisals arise. If Ricard is correct, what is truly you?"

Let there be silence as students digest the point. Students might easily skip over the importance of the *quality* of mind in favor of the *object* of awareness. Then, ask the class to close their eyes for a second and mindfully notice what they're feeling or thinking.

"Daniel Goleman quotes a researcher who says that anger 'is the mood people are worst at controlling.'[27] Do you agree?" Give students the space to respond.

"What is the 'ventilation fallacy'? What is your response to Daniel Goleman's discussion of the fallacy?"

The ventilation fallacy is thinking you must express everything you feel, and expression will diminish or destroy the anger. But it doesn't. Ask students how they usually feel after yelling at someone.

It can be difficult for students to differentiate not venting and suppressing. They might imagine expressing or suppressing anger are their only choices. But isn't "how you do it" important? "What are positive ways to express anger?"

Matthieu Ricard says kindness can be an antidote to anger. If you feel kind or loving, you won't intentionally harm others.[28] But what does this mean? You can't just think kind thoughts and chase away anger. *"If you could be kind consciously, on purpose, is that kindness fake?"* students often wonder.

Think of the implications of the question. "Does being conscious mean being fake? Why be mindful, then? Why be awake at all? To be kind, instead of feeling you are wrong, deficient, or under attack, or someone else is wrong, take a slow breath and listen to yourself. Explore what is there without judging or attacking. It is not just when you meditate that you can practice kindness. It is in class, at home, on the street that you learn how to be kind."

Science classes, especially chemistry and biology, when discussing hormones, neurotransmitters, or genetics might give the impression that the chemical and electrical interactions of the brain create automatic reactions that preclude free will, or preclude learning to be kind. Maybe kind people are just born that way? Question the logic and way of thinking underlying this assumption.

"In informal logic, there is a fallacy called a 'category mistake.' Do you know what that is?" Probably, no one will speak up. To speak about atoms is one level of discourse about reality; chemicals and emotions other levels. You can say, "My adrenalin decided I should fight," but you would, hopefully, be speaking metaphorically.

"Free will has been debated for thousands of years. What does neuroplasticity 'say' about free will? Since meditation can strengthen the insula so you are more prepared to act for the welfare of others,[29] does this mean meditation makes you more or less free? And what does free will mean? Is freedom the same as having no restraints on your actions? Are you free if every time you have a thought or desire, you act it out? Would you feel free then? Aren't there thoughts that you have that you never want to put into action? If so, then how do you decide what thought to act on? If you can act on one thought and not another, then you have some control, don't you?"

And maybe you are using the word "think" in ambiguous ways. There is "think" as in "have thoughts," and think as in notice, consider, and reflect. When you notice the thought that someone is disrespecting you, or you feel wronged, take a breath. Consider what is occurring and how to respond. *NBC: Notice, Breathe, and Consider.*

When you feel wronged, who do you feel is in charge, you or the other? You can feel someone else has the power and you want it back. The very flow of your consciousness can be disturbed. You no longer feel whole.[30] You become what Martin Buber called "I-It."[31] The other person relates to you and you relate to yourself as an "it." You are always the primary victim of your anger. Is it easier to hurt an "it" or a "thou"?

With mindfulness, free will takes on an interesting meaning. Mindfulness helps dissolve ongoing emotions, moods and the stories you tell yourself. Your mind clears. In Taoism there is a principle called "Wu Wei" or "acting without acting," acting without deliberate planning.[32] When acting with Wu Wei, there is no "free will" because there is no distinct thing called will, and no story; the person is so integrated with the situation that it is the situation itself that wills and the situation acts.

Ask students, "What are ways to intervene in your own anger?"

Discuss creating a gap between your triggers and responses. *NBC: Notice, Breathe, and Consider.* Notice your thoughts and feelings. Take three breaths. Challenge your thoughts and consider what they might mean and what options you have for a response. Ask yourself if the actions you feel driven to take are appropriate.

If the anger you experience is not at an immediate and dangerous situation, you can pull back, do something engaging, go to the gym and let the intensity of feeling dissipate. You can place yourself in the other person's situation in order to better understand why she did what she did and meet anger with kindness. The Dalai Lama suggests that when someone does something you feel is wrong or hurtful, separate the actor from the action. The action is what is hurtful. Don't think of the actor as unforgivable or evil, but work on educating the person about the consequences of the action itself.[33]

Table 3.2   Chart for Analyzing the Components of Emotion.

Emotion:		
Sensations: What do you feel?	Thoughts and Images	Actions:
Location:		What is the evolutionary use of the emotion?
Quality:		
Intensity:		What action do you feel impelled to take?
Physiology:	Psychology:	Interventions:

To end the class, discuss diagraming the components of anger. (See table 3.2) "When you're home, in order to pull together all that you've learned about anger, make a chart of its components. Write down what triggers anger. In the first column, record the physiology of anger—what goes on inside you, what sensations do you feel, where do they arise in your body, and what physiological changes lead to those sensations? What does anger "feel like" to you? In the second column, record the thoughts and stories that go on in your mind and the psychological explanations for those thoughts. In the third, record, what are the evolutionary uses for anger, what actions you imagine taking. And record interventions that you think will work with you."

"Take time to contemplate anger and what often results from it. Explore your own experiences. Are there stories that come up whenever you get angry? Can you find any patterns to your feelings? Treat your stories like clues to the mystery of yourself. The book of yourself is a great book. Learn from it. Enjoy it."

As a teacher, you need to remember to consult or recommend students speak with support staff, especially if students show persistent alienation, anger, anxiety, depression, and similar emotions.

LESSON SIXTEEN: JOY AND FEAR

Readings to Give Background for Discussion

- Paul Ekman, *Emotions Revealed*, 152–171.
- Daniel Goleman, *Emotional Intelligence*, 297–300.

When fear arises in a class, due to a test, one student's response to another student's actions, or a news event, make the conscious intent to face the fear sensitively and directly, with as much skill and compassion as you can bring to it. Obviously, fear can be a difficult subject to study in school. You have to be careful about bringing up deeply troubling memories. One way to start the discussion is first exploring joy. After greeting the students, ask them to be seated and begin mindfulness practice.

The Practice

"Let your mind and body settle down. Take a breath in, and then out. Just be easy on yourself. With your next breath, let your eyes close partially or fully. Relax into the breath and let your awareness follow it."

Pause to let students follow the breath on their own for a few seconds.

"What does the word 'joy' bring up for you? What images come to mind, or feelings? Allow the memory or idea of a joyous moment to come to mind. Or allow joyous words to come to you. What were you doing when you felt joyous? What did it feel like? Breathe in and feel what it is like to breathe joy. You can even say to yourself: 'I breathe in joy.' Breathe out and say to yourself: 'I breathe out in joy.' Just breathe in and feel the moment of joy arise inside you. And breathe out in joy. Is joy energetic or lethargic? Is it light and open, or heavy? Notice how, when you feel joy, the world feels just right as it is. Just breathe it in and breathe it out. Sit for a moment with the feeling or idea of joy."

Ring the bell. Then ask students to take out their journals and answer the following questions:

1. What words, feelings, memories came to you when you imagined joy?
2. How do you recognize fear? Where do you feel it?

After a few minutes of writing, ask:

- "What came up for you about joy?"
- "What is joy like?"
- "Could you maintain the feeling?"

- "Why do we have joy? What is its use?"
- Students often respond that it gives you hope, probably helps you want to survive, and makes you feel more open to others, attentive, energetic.

Buddha's Brain points out joy is linked to the release of dopamine and activating the left prefrontal cortex, all of which helps your mind transfer skills and information from short-term memory to long-term memory.[34]

"Now let's switch to fear. What is the use of fear?" Fear can signal danger but also result in feeling helpless or at the mercy of something or someone. The flight-fight response is really a flight-fight-freeze response. We can feel helpless against or unable to handle whatever is coming, as in saying, "I'm frozen by fear."

"How do you know you are afraid? What are the signs?" The sensations students might mention include sweating, trembling in your legs and knees, and your heart starts beating rapidly.[35] By coming to realize the physiology and sensation of fear, students more easily realize how to intervene in the emotion. From recognizing that trembling legs can indicate fear, they realize that running on a treadmill can reduce fear.

"What does a fearful face look like?" Students, more or less seriously, will try to show the face of fear. Their eyes get this open yet terrified, focused look. Their jaw drops open. Fear can wake you up, keep you from drifting off into fantasy or chase you into a fantasy. If joy means everything is all right, fear is everything is not all right. It can ready you to run, but there's a link between fear, or feeling something is not right, and anger. "Raise your hand if you sometimes get angry when you're afraid?" Watch for their response.

"What point of time does fear usually orient us toward?" Fear centers attention on the idea or the possibility of something negative happening in the future.

Fear readies you to run. When angry, blood flows to your hands, so you can fight. When you're afraid, blood flows to your feet. That's one reason why your feet tremble and your heart races. But you might feel too scared to run. Instead of building a shell and pushing life away, you might get angry in order to run or fight well. Paul Ekman's research seems to confirm this. He says fear and anger can follow each other closely. And you react differently when a fear is immediate rather than impending. Ekman discusses three differences in the feeling of fear which arise, depending on the timing of a fearful event[36:]

1. An immediate threat that you then act on (with flight, for example) versus one that leads to extended worry and increased vigilance and tension.
2. The reduction of pain can follow an immediate threat, while an impending one, in which you worry, leads to increased pain.

3. The immediate and the impending fears involve different parts of the brain. If you do something about the fear, and take action, you no longer feel it as fear. If you think you are helpless or can't act, this leads not only to fear but also to terror.

"The object you fear does not by itself cause fear. As with anger, the story you tell yourself about the object and how confident you feel, influences your emotional response. Did you ever get angry with yourself for feeling fear? Raise your hand if you did." Wait for hands to be raised and acknowledge them.

"Don't people fear looking afraid? Did you ever *fear* fear?" Allow this to sink in. A strong sense of fear includes fearing fear. Maybe we get angry to make fear go away. But there are exceptions. Many people seem to like being afraid in certain situations, as in the movies or amusement rides. Any form of art, even horror films, can be enjoyed for the fear, terror, and other emotions they invoke.

The ancient Greeks valued staged tragic dramas. They thought they uplifted them. The theory was that tragedy provided a way to work out emotions in the theater and so they don't work them out on other citizens.[37] Daniel Goleman theorized that horror movies might serve a similar function today. When you sit in a movie and survive the attack of the walking dead, your unconscious might be better prepared to face a stressful and frightening real situation.[38]

"Fear can spread out to include other aspects of a situation. What does fear do to the sense of presence?" When afraid, you can get so lost in what might occur that you forget what is occurring.[39] Emotion gives meaning to our expectations of the future and memories of the past, and thus set up the range of possibilities for *now*.

"How do you intervene in or let go of fear?"

Students often mention exercise and laughter. "Can you laugh without being present? Fear involves a projection into a scary future. Thus, the more you settle into awareness of the present, the less you feel or fear *fear*. When you allow yourself to just feel, you then feel *allowing*, open. The fear changes into something else. You need to fear fear in order to prolong it, to feel it in order to transform it. When fear arises, take three breaths, observe your situation carefully, and ask yourself: 'Does the situation I am in require me to act? How?' Chart the components of fear in order to lessen fear."

LESSON SEVENTEEN: UNDERSTANDING AND LETTING GO OF ANXIETY

Readings for Class Discussion

• Daniel Goleman, *Emotional Intelligence*, 65–69.

• Reread Hanson, *Buddha's Brain*, 49–63.

What is anxiety and how can you decrease it? The level of anxiety in schools has been increasing noticeably. Many families feel stressed economically. Schools cannot afford to ignore this. Instead, economics and social studies classes can discuss how certain political and social situations lead to economic hardship and inequality. English classes can read novels and biographies of people facing economic and other forms of hardship. Teachers in any subject can help students understand and decrease the anxiety and stress they feel. One way to begin a lesson on how to skillfully face your own anxiety is to practice an inquiry into courage and feeling that whatever comes up, you can deal with it.

The Practice

Direct students to take a moment and settle into their seat. "Place your attention on your forehead and feel the breath from that part of your body. Notice the very subtle sense of your forehead breathing in and breathing out. Now, put your attention on your shoulders. You might notice, with the next in breath, how your shoulders rise with the in breath, and let go, settle down with the out breath. It is easier to feel how the body breathes by focusing on the shoulders, how they expand with the in breath, and let go with the out breath, isn't it? Let the sense of simply breathing in and out center you, calm you."

"Let come to mind the word courage and the character of courage. Was there a time that you ever acted courageously or witnessed or read about such an action? What was the action? Was it facing a fear? Acting selflessly? Acting to aid others? What does courage mean to you or what words come to mind when you think of courage? What do you think it feels like to act with courage?" Pause for a second.

"What does it feel like to realize you can face whatever arises in your life? Just sit for a moment with the feeling of courage."

In a few moments, ring the singing bowl. Write the following journal questions on the board for students to consider:

1. What came up for you about courage?
2. What does anxiety or worry "feel like?" Where do you feel it?

After students write for a few minutes, ask: "What came up for you when you thought of courage?"

Courage can be exhilarating. But it can also bring up memories of when you were less than courageous. Students might find it difficult to separate out what they really feel from all the media images of guns blazing, of knights and monsters. Courageous actions don't have to be dramatic. Simply facing what you hold in memory, being genuine, and not trying to please other people can be courageous.

Then, turn the discussion to the components of worry and anxiety. "Where do you feel worry? What does worry feel like? How do you know you are worried?" Students may respond:

- *"I feel caught, that my heart is in someone else's hands."*
- *"I feel queasy; my stomach clenches and won't let go."*
- *"When I worry, I play out all the possible bad things that might happen in a specific situation."*
- *"When I worry, I imagine my sense of self will be badly shaken."*

Continue the analysis with the following questions:

- "Where have you seen similar responses before?" Which emotions have a similar physiological response as worry?
- "What triggers worry?"
- "Are worry and anxiety the same?"

Center the class solely on worry. "What might be the use of worry?" Listen and discuss student responses. They might discuss preparing you for an event or motivating you to be vigilant. Worry illustrates the power of the human brain. Only a species with a great ability to imagine different futures can worry. When you worry, you imaginatively explore possible consequences or implications of an action. The fearful component gives the exercise weight, makes you take notice.

However, worry can go beyond, even negate, its evolutionary use of helping to motivate you to prepare and be vigilant, and become an addiction or habitual way of living. It can become an underlying pattern of doubting your own ability to meet a situation and turn nervousness or stress into something more afflictive.

"Did you ever notice how worry can be like magical thinking? Without being conscious of it, your way of thinking implies, 'If I worry, then it won't happen.' But is it true that worry will stop an event you dread from occurring?" Listen to student responses.

Next, switch the discussion to anxiety.

- "What sensations signal anxiety?"
- "What does anxiety feel like?"
- "How is it different from worry?"

Listen to and possibly record on the board student responses.

When you are anxious, the sympathetic nervous system, which deals with perceived threats, turns on. Appetite turns off. [40] Thoughts speed up. "What thoughts do you have when anxious?" Students often report that anxious thoughts move quickly and repeat over and over. The world seems darker. They might feel imprisoned or that they will never have the chance to be fully alive. Or they might feel unable to discern the right choice between two or more possibilities. They feel pushed to label or define themselves as inadequate to face what might occur, as if having a label, even a painful one, will provide a sense of continuity and control.

It is important for students to realize that their way of thinking and responding to anxious feelings and thoughts can decrease the anxiety they feel. Research shows that pain interpreted as externally generated is rated as more unpleasant than pain thought of as internally generated.[41]

"What are interventions in anxiety?" Students often mention awareness, interrupting the cycle of emotion by swimming, working out at the gym, seeing an inspiring movie or doing something to relax, like taking a walk. They might recognize that when the atmosphere at home is one of safety, trust, and acceptance, anxiety decreases.

And each time you compassionately help others or engage in exercise, sport, dance, martial arts, or other artistic endeavors, and do it with focused attention, for the sense of beauty, the aliveness of the act itself, not for a grade or to please others, you reduce your anxiety. You do it to feel the timing of the music, the rhythm of moving your body, the sound of a poem—for the value of the activity itself.[42] The act of allowing yourself to be fully present in your actions proclaims to yourself and the world that your life has value.

When you feel worry and anxiety, you might feel like isolating yourself. Instead, develop a plan of action to confront and rationally deal with whatever event is coming up that triggers anxiety, and discuss the plan with others. Taking action reduces anxiety. Remember: Worry and anxiety oversensitive you to think of stimuli as threatening and to create a story with you as the loser. As *Buddha's Brain* points out, once you feel stress, and life is "on simmer," ready to boil, it is easy to imagine that at any moment, a threat can arrive.[43] You fear the moment, feel the challenge is too big to face, and thus increase it. So, question your thoughts and the story you weave with them. Chart the components of anxiety and worry.

Many people grow up thinking that if you feel good, you are missing something, and you are not perceptive or smart enough to realize it. You can be conditioned to feel that you don't deserve happiness. Matthieu Ricard shares an anecdote about a successful American friend of his. When asked by friends what she wanted to do with her life, she said she wanted to be happy. The response was an embarrassed silence.[44] Denigration of happiness makes you more vulnerable to anxiety and more easily manipulated by others. Why this happens in countries like the United States can make for an engaging discussion. To intervene in anxiety and worry, take action. Solve problems and engage in activities that help you feel good about your abilities.

LESSON EIGHTEEN: GREED AND HUMAN HISTORY

In a history class on World War II, or on the first known wars in ancient Sumeria, visualization and mindfulness practices can be used to reveal how human psychology and emotion is at the root of historical events. How could it not be? A science class on biology, evolution, or human nature can be enhanced by a direct study of one's own nature, or an economics course enhanced by a direct inquiry into one's own economic practices.

Is the economy driven by "invisible market forces" or by a sense of human need? The causes of war are often oversimplified in school texts and discussions. How does such a massive event as a war happen? Is war somehow prescribed by "human nature"? What roles do greed, fear, and hatred or a sense of social inequity and oppression play in war? Discussions of such questions can make for a dynamic and meaningful education.

The Practice

Greet students. Once they are seated, introduce today's practice. It will be an inquiry into what greed is, and how to diminish it.

"Settle yourself in your chair. Maybe close your eyes. Breathe out, until you feel most of the air is gone. Then let your belly relax and expand, inhale on its own. Breathe out, and then notice that the inhalation happens by itself. It doesn't need your conscious help."

"As you inhale, allow your mind to think of the word greed. What comes up for you? What words or images come to mind, or maybe a person? Did you ever think someone you knew, or someone you read about or saw in a movie, was acting greedily? Who was it? What marked the action as greedy? How did the greedy action affect you or other people?"

"Have you ever felt greed? What made your yearning for something feel like greed? What were you greedy for? Was there something you thought you just had to have? Maybe you saw something online, or in a store. And you felt, 'I need that.' What did you think would occur if you had whatever it was you wanted? How would having this object or whatever change your life? How would the greed affect how you related with others?"

"Now, imagine feeling just fine the way you are. Maybe you normally feel this way. Maybe, you were out in a park on a beautiful day, the sun on your face, and you felt relaxed, happy. All you needed was the sense of the sun on your face, nothing else. Or you were talking with friends and you felt life was good. You felt complete and alive, in the moment. Just feel this for a moment. Just feel the sense of completion. You are fine as you are and can do what needs to be done. Your life has beauty, love, and meaning. There's nothing you have to add to yourself, nothing missing. Just sit with feeling that right now you are full and good."

Ring the singing bowl.

"What did it feel like to want something you don't have?" Students often reply that it hurts to feel like that. It reminds them of the class on suffering or anxiety. This practice could be used to introduce the lesson on psychological suffering.

- "What thoughts arise when you feel greed?"
- "What affect, if any, did greed have on your breathing?" Buried in greed is often a sense that without possessing whatever it is you desire, you might not be able to take another breath.
- "Is jealousy or envy the same as greed?" Students often connect greed with jealousy or envy, which add a twist to greed.
- "What is the difference between jealousy and envy? Is there a difference?"

Greed can lead to disliking yourself. It might mask anger. It is usually thought of as a form of grasping or clinging to possessions, external signs of power or wealth. But it is also a form of aversion, pushing people away. You cling to the external and push away empathy, compassion. You dislike feeling there's something you lack.

You can feel greed not only about possessions, but also about knowledge and information. Ask students if they ever noticed this in school or with Facebook and other social media. You see someone's page and think, "Wow. I don't have that." Or, "I didn't know that." And you feel bad, that there is something wrong with you, because you did not know it. You can distort how you see others by looking for what you can get from them. A student once dramatically said, *"When you worry so much about what others think of you, it hollows you out. You become a Zombie. You feel empty inside and you use others to try to fill you up."*

When you feel envy, your attention is focused on someone else, or what someone else has or does. A student described it as, "You feel lessened by her success or lower than her. You think of yourself compared to her. It's selfishness turned into a put down of yourself." Compliment students on such insights. Anxiety is inherent in grasping. You might feel you hate that someone else has what you don't have. But it might not be hate. You might want to *be* the other person. One student said, *"That's what gets me. I hate that I'm not her. I hate that I don't have that life and the freedom she has."*

With jealousy, you excessively watch what others have and fear losing what you do have. Paul Ekman says jealousy is not one emotion but more of a scene involving three actors (the person sought after, the rival, and the seeker) and several emotions.[45] Notice how greed, envy, and jealousy involve your sense of identity, your sense of lack, or of seeking.

- "What purposes could greed, jealousy or envy serve?"
- "What examples, if any, can you give of a positive use for greed, jealousy or envy?"

Many will consider these emotions a perversion of having a goal, a purpose, or striving. But might envy wake you up to injustice? Or might jealousy wake you to the fact that you care about someone? If you wake up to greed, it can reveal a desire to improve your life or possibly reveal what you value and where you are placing your sense of self.

"Does greed help you survive—or hurt your chances?" Ayn Rand[46] and Adam Smith[47] argue that only if you think of your own interest first will everyone's interest be served. Selfishness is good for everyone. You help others only because it is in your interests to do so.

Ask students: "Do you love someone only out of self-interest, only for what the other person gives you? Is love about using others?" Have students take a moment to notice their own feelings. The discussion of selfishness often raises the level of anxiety in the classroom. The students' emotional response to the question is important evidence for a possible conclusion.

"How do you intervene in greed or envy? How do you stop it?"

You need to feel the other person has feelings, thoughts, like you do. You stop the hollowing out process. You fill yourself with awareness. You are happy, grateful for their happiness. When you are compassionate, caring you feel like you have something to give. You feel valuable. When you are selfish, and think of yourself in terms of what you own or control, you can feel hollow. You can't solve psychological or spiritual problems, like those caused by greed, only with a material solution.

After the lesson on emotion, turn to the historical material of the lesson. "Let's apply our analysis of greed to better understand large-scale historical events. We were talking about possible reasons Germany started World War II. What factors push people to war and violence? Were the Germans trying to solve a psychological or spiritual problem with a war?[48] Do people go to war or fight to find a sense of purpose and meaning?"[49]

Over the next few days, as you continue this discussion and analysis and get immersed in material on the causes and conditions that might have led to the war, be aware of the large philosophical and moral questions. Is any war justifiable? Was the war unstoppable? What does the presence of war say about human nature? If you assume something about your nature, you act in accord with that assumption. To talk about human nature is to talk about who you are as a person, as a friend or loved one, parent or child. It is not just an abstract question. Your answer affects the way you live your life.

Teachers, as well as students, need to uncover the larger dimensions and implications of the questions that arise with the material of the course. For example, if, in a history class, you overemphasize the horrors that humans have perpetrated and leave out the good, or see the good as inconsequential, banal, and the awful as "that's just the way it is." If you talk about Hitler and forget Asoka[50] and some of the great humanitarians or saints. Then I recommend you rethink what you are teaching. The everyday cooperation humans experience buying food, riding a bus, or discussing material in a classroom is not "inconsequential," but the most consequential. It is often the cooperation you experience every day that makes it possible to notice evil. You might claim to value compassion and have empathy for your students. Yet, if you teach that selflessness is a myth, that all of us are born to put competitiveness and greed before compassion and love, you undermine that claim.

Especially when the subject is difficult, you need to hold the reality, even the difficult and painful reality, in your arms for a second; to listen to what is said by a student or inside yourself, without jumping to a conclusion or running to hide. You need to let the light in. The question of what it means to be a human being is a crucial question for students to raise and for teachers to address directly. Hidden in the question is the recognition that *who you are* is about *who you choose to be*. Who do you choose to be? What do you choose to teach?

NOTES

1. David Loy, "Money, Sex, War, Karma." Lecture, Workshop from Omega Institute of Holistic Studies, Rhinebeck, NY, August 20, 2012.

2. Eugen Herrigel, *Zen in the Art of Archery* (New York: Vintage Books, 1953), 69.

3. Linda Lantieri and Daniel Goleman, *Building Emotional Intelligence: Techniques to Cultivate Inner Strength in Children* (Boulder, CO: Sounds True, 2008), 5–7.

4. Richard Davidson, "Emotions from the Perspective of Western Behavioral Science," in *The Dalai Lama at MIT*, eds. Anne Harrington and Arthur Zajonc (Cambridge, MA: Harvard University Press, 2006), 143.

5. George Dreyfus, "An Abhidharmic View of Emotional Pathologies and Their Remedies," in *The Dalai Lama at MIT*, 118–119.

6. Goleman, *Emotional Intelligence*, 6.

7. Ibid., 6–8.

8. Joseph Chilton Pearce, *Evolution's End: Changing the Potential of Our Intelligence* (New York: HarperCollins Publishers, 1992), 42–43.

9. Paul Ekman, ed. *Emotional Awareness, Overcoming the Obstacles to Psychological Balance and Compassion* (New York: Henry Holt and Company, 2008), 68.

10. Ibid., 39.

11. Iain McGilchrist, *The Master and his Emissary: The Divided Brain and the Making of the Western World* (New Haven, CT: Yale University Press, 2009), 88.

12. Daniel Siegel, *The Developing Mind: How Relationships and the Brain Interact to Shape Who We Are* (New York: The Guilford Press, 2012), 148–185.

13. Paul Ekman, "On Emotional Triggers," in *Emotional Awareness, Overcoming the Obstacles to Psychological Balance and Compassion*, ed. Paul Ekman (New York: Henry Holt and Company, 2008), 38–39.

14. Ibid., 37–49.

15. Dacher Keltner, "Emotion," in *The Dalai Lama at MIT*, eds. Anne Harrington and Arthur Zajonc, (Cambridge, MA: Harvard University Press, 2006), 155.

16. Shinzen Young, "Break Through Difficult Emotions: How to Transform Painful Feelings with Mindfulness Meditation." Sounds True, CD, January 31, 2006.

17. Ibid, 57–58.

18. Goleman, *Emotional Intelligence*, 57.

19. William Shakespeare, *Hamlet*, eds. Barbara A. Mowat and Paul Werstine, (New York: Simon and Schuster, 1992), 3.2.77.

20. Roger Walsh, *Essential Spirituality: Exercises from the World's Religions to Cultivate Kindness, Love, Joy, Peace, Vision, Wisdom and Generosity* (New York: John Wiley & Sons, Inc., 1999), 90–91.

21. Mark Matousek, *Ethical Wisdom: What Makes Us Good* (New York: Doubleday, 2011), 74.

22. Paul Ekman, *Emotions Revealed: Recognizing Faces and Feelings to Improve Communication and Emotional Life* (New York: Times Books, 2003), 174.

23. Davidson, "Emotions from the Perspective of Western Science," 148.

24. Ekman, *Emotional Awareness*, 109.

25. Ibid, 116.

26. Ricard, *The Dalai Lama at MIT*, 153.

27. Goleman, *Emotional Intelligence*, 59.

28. Ricard, *The Dalai Lama at MIT*, 159.

29. David DeSteno, "The Morality of Meditation," *New York Times Sunday Review*, July 7, 2013, 12.

30. Albert Low, *Creating Consciousness: A Study of Consciousness, Creativity, Evolution, and Violence* (Ashland, OR: White Cloud Press), 209–213.

31. Martin Buber, *I and Thou, 2nd Edition* (New York: Charles Scribner's Sons, 1958), 3–9.

32. Benjamin Hoff, *The Tao of Pooh* (New York: Penguin Books, 1982), 67–90.

33. Ekman, *Emotional Awareness*, 41, 109.

34. Hanson, *Buddha's Brain*, 198.

35. Ekman, *Emotions Revealed*, 160–169.

36. Ibid., 155–156.

37. Hubert Dreyfus and Sean Kelly, *All Things Shining: Reading the Western Classics to Find Meaning in a Secular Age* (New York: Free Press, 2011), 98–102.

38. Daniel Goleman, *Social Intelligence: The New Science of Human Relationships* (New York: Bantam Books, 2006), 184–186.

39. Albert Low, *Creating Consciousness*, 213.

40. Ron Leifer, M. D., *The Happiness Project: Transforming the Three Poisons that Cause the Suffering We Inflict on Ourselves and Others* (Ithaca, NY: Snow Lion Press, 1997) 99.

41. David J. Linden, *Touch: The Science of Hand, Heart, and Mind* (New York: Viking, 2015), 168.

42. Mihalyi Csikszentmihalyi, *Flow: The Psychology of Optimal Experience* (New York: Harper Collins, 1990), 68–69.

43. Hanson, *Buddha's Brain*, 55–57.

44. Mathieu Ricard, *Happiness: A Guide to Developing Life's Most Important Skill* (New York: Little Brown and Company, 2003), 17.

45. Ekman, *Emotions Revealed*, 217.

46. Ayn Rand, *The Virtue of Selfishness: Centennial Edition* (New York: Signet, 1964).

47. See David R. Loy, *A Buddhist History of the West: Studies in Lack* (Albany, NY: SUNY Press, 2002), 156–160.

48. See Ibid., 94–104, 211–215.

49. For an engaging discussion on creating meaning and the mythic quality of war, see Lawrence LeShan, *The Psychology of War: Comprehending its Mystique and its Madness* (New York: Helios Press, 2002), 77–83.

50. Ashoka was the King who united India, renounced war, and adopted Buddhism. See Robert Thurman, *Inner Revolution: Life, Liberty, and the Pursuit of Real Happiness* (New York: Riverhead Books, 1998), 109–133.

Chapter 4

Emotions of Opening and Approach

After studying anger, fear, and worry, it should be clear that emotions are too complex to easily categorize. It has been tried. Emotions have been categorized in many ways, as painful versus pleasurable, negative versus positive—ones expressing suffering versus ones indicating the relief of suffering. There are prosocial emotions, which open you to others, to learning, and to observing the world more completely. And there are those where you attack (hate), turn away (depression), or are neutral (disinterest).

However, is love always joyful? Is anger always painful? Love can be an opening to at least one person, and can either distort or clarify your observations and thinking. You might expect love to always be an experience of opening. Yet, to feel open, you need to push away fear, so sometimes fear leaps out from behind love. Fear and many forms of love can be two sides of one shifting mental state. Emotion is dynamic. It is not something you can hold in your hands and admire. It is more akin to *how* you hold anything and *how* you touch anyone, more of a multifaceted process than a distinct entity.

Kindness and joy are two emotions of opening introduced in chapter 3. Compassion, empathy, and love will be the subject of this chapter.

LESSON NINETEEN: WHAT IS EMPATHY AND COMPASSION?

Readings for Discussion

- V. S. Ramachandran, *The Tell-Tale Brain: A Neuroscientist's Quest for What Makes Us Human* (New York: W. W. Norton & Co., 2011), 116–135.
- Christian Jarrett, "A Calm Look at the Most Hyped Concept in Neuroscience—Mirror Neurons," *Brain Watch/Wired*, December 13, 2013: http://www.wired.com/2013/12/a-calm-look-at-the-most-hyped-concept-in-neuroscience-mirror-neurons/

Compassion is something you teach mostly by modeling and practicing it. To teach compassion, use the classroom as an opportunity to be compassionate. Study how to learn from whatever happens and to treat students as mentors, to each other and to you. How are you like your students and your students like you? When a student misbehaves or has difficulty learning, it's easy to feel defensive or at fault. When you have a quiet moment, hold an image of the face of the student in your mind. Just let it sit for a moment and imagine what he or she might be feeling. The simple act of calmly holding and accepting readies the mind and heart for insight. And ask the same of students.

Ramachandran's discussion of mirror neurons and empathy in *The Tell-Tale Brain* can lead to an engaging discussion in a biology, social studies, or an English class.

- "Are what neuroscientists call 'mirror neurons' almost too good to be true? They have been used to explain so much of human experience, from empathy to imagination and story-telling, to the conversations we have with ourselves in our mind."
- "Is empathy different from compassion?"

"The psychologist Paul Ekman studied emotion and facial expression. Did you ever watch the television show, *Lie To Me*? The show is based on Ekman and his work. He discusses three types of empathy: Cognition, Feeling, and Compassion."[1]

1. Cognition: an ability to discern the feelings of another, to "read" another person and the physical and action cues.
2. Emotional resonance: you feel a concern for or "feel with" another person. You feel distress over another person's suffering, unlike a sociopath, who can "read" another person but not feel anything or care.

3. Compassionate empathy: when the concern, care, or connection you feel for the well-being of another person drives you to act to reduce his or her suffering without losing yourself in the other person's emotion. Empathy by itself might mean a concern for others, but not necessarily motivate action.

The Practice

Let's explore compassion and empathy.

Many compassion practices start with giving compassion to *you* before giving it to others. To respect others, or have compassion for others, you must first have it for yourself. But many teens (and adults) fight self-compassion. They feel undeserving. To work through this gently, have students imagine compassion in general—compassionate words, gestures, actions, people. Then ask them to give this compassion to others who are suffering, first to someone close, ending with someone they've had trouble with. By giving to others, they find a way to give it to themselves.

"Take a moment to get comfortable. Settle your mind and allow yourself to turn within and listen to your breath, as you usually do with mindfulness practice. Hear the silence between the sounds and breaths."

"Let compassion come to mind. What images or words arise when you hear the word 'compassion'? Picture a compassionate person, someone either real or imagined, someone you actually know or met, or someone you just read about. What does she look like? How does she walk? How does she hold her head? Imagine her smile, how she talks. How does she move her hands?"

"Now, imagine someone you know, maybe a friend, someone you could easily relate to. Think of a moment or some discussion you had with the person. What might have been going on inside him or her? What might he be going through? Just feel along with him or her. Imagine compassion flowing from you to him or her, or concern, care, kindness. Or just wish him or her compassion. Maybe say to yourself, 'May this person be happy, healthy, and at peace.' Just say it. 'May this person be happy, healthy, and at peace.' And feel it, feel your concern, your care." If this is the first time you are doing this and have limited time, you might want to skip, now, to the last paragraph of the practice.

"Imagine someone you don't know well, maybe someone who might be suffering. Picture the last time you saw this person. How does he look, talk, act? Imagine bringing compassion, kindness to this person. Imagine feeling what he might be feeling, and caring about his welfare. Say to yourself, 'May this person be happy, healthy, and at peace.'"

"Then imagine someone you had a disagreement with. Picture the person or think of how the person looks, talks, acts. Think of the last time you saw this person. Now, imagine bringing compassion to this person. Imagine feeling what she might be feeling and caring about her welfare. Say to yourself, 'May this person be happy, healthy, and at peace.'"

"Then imagine giving compassion, kindness to others around you, or to everyone. Imagine everyone around you feeling cared for. And it goes both ways. Imagine giving this care to yourself. Say to yourself, 'May I be happy, healthy, and at peace.' Say it again. 'May I be happy, healthy, and at peace.' Imagine other people caring for you as you care for them. Just feel what it is like to care and be cared for. Rest in that feeling for a moment."

Ring the bell. There will probably be quiet for a moment as students stretch and process the practice. Ask about their experience and whether or not it was difficult for them. Listen and discuss their responses. The sense of feeling cared for can bring a student to tears, or create a sense of great joy. Ask students: "Which was easier—to feel compassion for yourself or for others?"

Research indicates that compassion practices increase the connectivity and coherence between different areas of the brain.[2] Ramachandran discusses new research on how people think and feel better about life and themselves when they act with compassion.[3]

Students often respond by asking, *"If compassion makes you feel better, does that mean that empathy or compassion are forms of selfishness?"* They might feel compassion is fake and you can't help being selfish. They might cite examples of people doing nothing when they see a person attacked. In such a situation, students might appear to react instead of respond and consider. Ask them to take a breath, notice what they feel, and then think about their responses to the question.

"What does your culture teach about compassion? What lessons from the media can you recall about compassion? Does watching football, for example, teach empathy?"

"Do you associate compassion with pity? Is there a difference between the two?" The two words can be similar in meaning, but are often understood very differently. Pity can mean sympathy, feeling sad about another person's pain, but at more of a distance. The root of pity is the Latin "pietas" or "piety" and students often hear in the word a feeling of obligation or placing yourself above the pitied person.

"Can you pay a price for compassion? Can compassion and empathy put you at risk? And, if so, can it be a form of selfishness?" To act with a sincere concern for another person's well-being, you might have to take risks or ignore other people's opinion of your action. Both pity and sympathy include feeling sad about another person's suffering. But with compassion, once you notice the other person's suffering and you feel concerned, even sad in response, you want to end that suffering just like you would want to end your own, even if it involves risk.

Hidy Ochiai, author and renowned educator in the fields of character education, self-development, and the traditional Japanese Martial Arts, gave an example of the price you can pay for compassion. In a karate class decades ago, he told a story of a student who came to class wanting to learn karate but couldn't walk more than a few steps without crutches and leg braces. Each time he tried to practice without crutches, he would fall after taking only a step or two. Every time the boy fell, Ochiai insisted that he get up on his own. Others criticized Ochiai for being heartless, but he was only giving the boy what was needed. After eight or nine months, the boy could walk unaided across the room doing blocks and punches. He eventually earned a brown belt.

Ochiai was crying inside as he watched the boy's struggles but had to keep his feelings to himself. This was an act of compassion. You can pay a tremendous price for it. But it is a prize above all others. If you do what appears to be a compassionate act in order to get money or recognition or to feel good about yourself, then it's not compassion and you do not get the benefits. Compassion includes "feeling as the other." Once you impose your own gain on that experience, you lose the "as" part; you lose the focus on the other. Hidy Ochiai even said compassion is beyond sympathy and empathy; it is, in a sense, to become the other person and act for that person's well-being.

Often, people ignore the suffering of others because they don't want to feel distress or concern or they are conditioned to not notice. If you can learn to not notice, you can learn to notice.

But how can you value another person so much you think from his or her perspective? This is where mirror neurons come in.

- What are mirror neurons?
- How do we know they exist? And if they exist, what do they explain about human experience and the possibility or limits of compassion?

Mirror neurons were discovered in the early 1990s. They are systems of neurons and not a specific type. A researcher named Giacomo Rizzolatti and his colleagues, while studying monkeys, discovered that "some of the neurons studied fired not only when the monkey performed an action, but also when it watched another monkey performing the same action." They were, possibly, "reading the other monkey's mind" or understanding another by having their own neurons fire almost as if they were doing the same action.[4] In other words, mirror neurons can be interpreted as saying we understand what another is feeling by feeling the same thing ourselves.[5]

Students often ask, *"How come they don't just repeat the action? What stops them?"* We have inhibitory cells, in our skin, joints and elsewhere that stop us from totally copying others.[6] They are in the skin to create a border, an outer limit to our sense of self and how much we usually feel, and to create a point of contact.[7] Skin is a boundary that makes touching possible.

"We know how compassion might be defined and that some people act compassionately. But do we need mirror neurons to explain that?" The article by Christian Jarrett critiques the common interpretation of the evidence. Ask students:

- "What are critiques of the mirror neuron theory?"
- "What proof other than Rizzolatti's experiments support the theory of mirror neurons?" Some commonly cited examples are yawning when you see someone else yawn, or a baby crying when it hears another baby cry. One way to learn is by imitation.
- "Do you think scientists are letting their theories about mirror neurons get ahead of their facts? Why or why not?"

If Ramachandran is correct, mirror neurons might help us better understand human thought. An orangutan has mirror systems. Imagine one swinging through the trees. She sees a branch and her mirror neurons enable her to picture and then feel the grasping of the branch and she does as she imagined. This same ability helps you think abstractly. If you can imagine and then feel the grasping of a branch, you can imagine philosophical theories and historical events and feel what it might be like to be there. You create a model in your mind of ways you can alter and modify what you see and test the implications of your model.[8] Students are often intrigued but skeptical about our present ways of understanding mirror neurons.

To sum up, ask:

- "What are the components of compassion? And how might mirror neurons advance our understanding of it?"
- "Is there a negative face of empathy?" Mirror neurons make empathy possible—and emotional contagion. You see someone hurt and your own pain or mirror networks turn on almost as if you were the person hurt.[9] However, contagion is when you pick up the pain, joy—or hate—of others without even realizing it. You enter a room, catch the anger of people there, and act angrily without awareness of the source of the anger.
- With empathy, you feel the distress, suffering, and know the source.[10] Repeatedly feeling the suffering of others can lead you to resist feeling it again, to "empathy fatigue," and burnout. This can happen to people confronted daily by other people's suffering, like those in helping professions. It can happen to doctors, therapists—or teachers.

- "Why is it that compassion has psychological and other benefits?" When you feel compassion, you not only feel concern for the other,[11] but you are open, kind, present, even loving, and your sense of self is enlarged. The sections of the brain associated with positive emotion turn on. Instead of resistance and burnout, you get courage, strength of mind, and inner balance.[12]

Compassion makes valuable insights possible, in and out of the classroom. For example, at a funeral, it is easy to get caught up in your own emotion and be unable to respond to others in their grief. With compassion, you realize simply allowing yourself to care and feel along with another person can be enough.

As the class comes to an end, remind students that, as of now, the mirror neuron systems, and our explanations of compassion and empathy in terms of those systems, are still theoretical, but their benefit to us is very real. Have students take a moment to record in their journal two components of compassion learned today.

LESSON TWENTY: WHAT IS LOVE?

Readings for Discussion

- Goleman, *Emotional Intelligence*, 129–147.
- Daniel Goleman, "A Recipe for Rapport," in *Social Intelligence: The New Science of Human Relationships* (New York: Bantam Dell, 2006). 27–37. (See also "The Neuroanatomy of a Kiss," 63–81; "Desire: His And Hers," 198–210.)
- Kent Berridge, in "Searching The Brain for Happiness," Dr. Morten Kringelbach, BBC News, May 2, 2006.

To start the lesson, ask the students to move the tables back and form the chairs into a circle. The aim is to create a sense of freshness and openness with no tables getting between you. And usually the students welcome this change. This day is important. There will always be students who meet the topic of love with skepticism, at best, or anger and hurt, and others will meet it with intense yearning. This is, of course, also true with teachers; some teachers say they can't teach about love.

What if a student says there is no such thing as love? What if she says love is a media invention—all hype. What if she claims that the media clearly distorts love? Movies, books, songs, advertisements often create unreal expectations and images, so you can start the class by talking about media images and bringing in examples to analyze. You can talk about lust versus love, and how love often hurts. Dig deep into the question of "What is love?"

To lead a mindfulness practice on love, you must recognize how emotional and complex the topic can be. You must know your students and what is appropriate for them. When you say love, follow with "caring" or "kindness." Remember that in leading a visualization or inquiry meditation, each word you say opens a world of emotion and memory. Let yourself be guided from your own connection with students and honesty with yourself. If you don't feel loving, don't lead this meditation; or tell the students that you, too, are confused about love, and hope to learn from the experience.

The Practice

"Today, we will do another reflective meditation. Such meditations are like throwing a stone into a lake and watching the ripples. When suggestions are made, simply allow them to spread out, and explore what you want of the ripples."

"Now close your eyes, settle down and turn attention inwards. Take a nice deep breath—then gently breathe out, letting go, relaxing your body as you go. Take another gentle breath, filling your belly; then let it go, and settle down, relax."

"Think about caring and loving, or someone acting in a caring and loving manner. Picture it in your mind. What comes up for you about loving care? What actions express this attitude? Just sit with that a second. If you want, think this to yourself: 'May I be happy, kind, and loving.'[13] Give yourself permission to think and feel these words. Then say them several times to yourself, with full awareness and concentration. 'May I be happy, kind, and loving.' Simply breathe in the feeling of you being happy—kind—loving. Breathe out and just settle into the feelings. Then listen. Listen to the acceptance or the rebellion. Listen to how you respond to the idea of allowing yourself to be happy, kind, loving—or loved. Listen and greet what arises with acceptance and love."

"Now think about other people. 'May others be happy, kind, loving.' Breathe in, 'May others be happy, kind, loving.' When you breathe out, just settle in your feeling of wishing care, kindness to another person. Notice which is easier—to wish love and caring for you, or for others? Which is more difficult? Just notice your response. And then sit for a moment with the sense of loving-caring."

Ring the bowl. Tell students to take a few minutes to record any thoughts, feelings, or images that came up while doing this practice. Then write:

- "What are your questions about love?"
- "Why is there such a concern and hype about it?"

Text Box 4.1 Is Love A Drug?

After reading the suggested BBC article or studying biology and how hormones and other chemicals direct behavior, students in my class often asked:

"Is love a drug?" asked Alex.
"What does it mean to you to say that 'love is a drug'?" I asked.
"It means that it's just a chemical response in the body," replied Alex.
"It means to me that you can get addicted to it. I think it is saying that our romantic thoughts are delusions," added Germaine.
"That would imply that love is not something you do but something done to you," said Sage. "What about other emotions—are they drugs, too? Why restrict ourselves to emotions—are sensations drugs? Thoughts?"
Good questions. Do you usually speak about hormones making choices, getting angry or falling in love?"

Text Box 4.2 Love and the Desire for Commitment and Security.

When asked "What else is included in love?" students in my class responded:

"When you are in love, there is a desire for safety, for security. You want a great deal of time together, not just one moment," said Sage.
"The Disney fairytale of riding off into the sunset together," Audrey added.
"And to protect the loved one. But what if they can't bear the vulnerability," added Sage, thinking through each word. "We want safety, care, commitment, time—but these desires can fight love."
"You can be so concerned with not getting hurt that you do nothing emotionally," Carlotta agreed. "I know people who refuse to get married because they fear the excitement of love would be lost by too much familiarity."

Ask students to share what they wrote in response to: "What are your questions and what do you want to learn about love?" You can have the students share in small groups or as a whole class. Student responses often include: *"Why do we want love so badly?" "Is it just a chemical reaction or a socially induced trance?" "Why do I get attracted to bums?" "How do you know if love is real?"*

Ask the students where to start the discussion. They often start with: "Why do you feel love? What purposes can it serve?" Listen for student responses.

A scientist named Harry Harlow[14] did an experiment with three groups of chimps. One group received no love or care. Another group was placed in a cage with an artificial mother. The third group was raised with their real mother. The artificial chimp was a wire mesh figure with fake hair and, instead of breasts, had two baby bottles for milk. The first group died in a year. The second group survived but had a high level of physical and emotional problems.[15] The third group grew up to be physically and emotionally healthy. Love is thus important for mental health and physical survival. "Is love merely something many species evolved in order for the species to survive? Is it something more than sexual attraction?" Let students share their analysis.

Remind students about an earlier discussion of the fallacy, in informal logic, called a "category mistake." To speak about atoms is one level of discourse about reality, chemicals and emotions are other levels.

Then begin unpacking the emotion directly. "Does loving someone make you vulnerable?" Listen and discuss student responses.

The vulnerability of love is often interpreted as painful. Students are concerned about the pain that love can bring. They notice how vulnerability can make you aggressive or you might try to limit vulnerability by controlling the person you love.

"If you are willing to be open and vulnerable, is that the same as valuing the person highly? Is this what pulls people together?" Or drives them apart?

Note that there is more to love than valuing and vulnerability. "What else is included in love?"

Love is dynamic. It is living with an edge. It is the vulnerability or openness of love that makes it exciting, yet without commitment and care, is it real? When you feel loved as a teenager, you feel you have made it, struck gold. But whose gold have you uncovered? Students usually leave this class deep in conversation.

LESSON TWENTY-ONE: WHAT ATTRACTS ONE PERSON TO ANOTHER?

If you can spend a second day on love, do so. You could easily spend a quarter of the year on the subject. On the second day, once again pull the tables out of the way. Start by having the whole class stand up in the open space.

The Practice

"Stand with your feet about shoulder width apart, eyes closed or mostly closed. Let your shoulders be relaxed. Breathe in and feel the air entering your nose. Exhale and feel the air going out." Go slowly, pausing between areas of the body.

"Breathe in and feel the air with your face, the nerves of the skin. Feel the temperature, the consistency. Breathe out, and let your face, your cheeks relax, let go. Put your attention on your jaw and breathe in, feeling the air as you breathe in. And as you exhale, let your jaw relax, settle down."

"Then put your attention on your shoulders. Feel your shoulders expand, take in air—and as you exhale, relax, settle down, let go of tension. Breathe into your belly, feeling your belly expand with the in breath—and let go, settle down with the out breath. Now, breathe all the way down to your toes. Breathe in and feel your body, thighs, feet expand; breathe out, and feel your body let go of tension and stand comfortably, with a sense of ease."

"Now feel all around you. Feel it with your feet. Feel it with your back, your face. Feel the air with your hands, its temperature, and consistency. Sense yourself being held by the air, touched by the air, and surrounded by this life giving substance. Then sense where you are standing. Picture where everyone and everything is in the room. Who is near you? Who is across the room? Then, gently, take a breath. Open your eyes and look around you. Is the room as you imagined? Are the other people in the class where you pictured them?"

Afterward, ask students: "How many of you accurately pictured the room in your imagination? Who could identify not only the people standing next to you, but others across the room?" This practice can be used at any time in the year. If you can go to a large room without furniture, you could even have students walk slowly and carefully around with eyes closed. This practice can be used early in the year, to break students from their phone and social media attachment.

After everyone is seated, continue the discussion of love.

- "What triggers one person to love another?"
- "Do you find yourself pulled to people who are like you, different from you or some balance between the two?"

Bring in a story, for example, *The Symposium*, written by the philosopher Plato, that can mirror back to students their thoughts and emotions. In *The Symposium*, the playwright Aristophanes tells the story of the original human being, a hermaphrodite, with four arms, four legs, two heads, and both male and female attributes. The gods, fearing the power of this being, split it in two. Forever after, the two halves try to reconnect and become whole again. This, says Aristophanes, is the story of love. Love is looking for your "other half," to reconnect what was rent asunder. Ask students if the story rings true to them?[16]

The story can sound beautiful, but what does it imply about human beings? Are you incomplete without another person to make you whole?

Text Box 4.3   Socrates on the Nature of Love.

In my class, I continued Plato's story about Socrates.

"Socrates doesn't agree with Aristophanes. He says the lovers: 'are seek-ing neither for the half, nor for the whole.'* What we seek, in love, he says, is to give birth to the good and the beautiful."
"What does that mean?" asked Carlotta.
"By 'giving birth to the good,' maybe he's saying that love is good; it's something we are responsible for," said Sage.
"Good," I replied, to some laughter. "We don't have the whole text here, only a few lines, so we might be totally off. But compare Socrates and Aristophanes. What is Aristophanes emphasizing?"
"Finding your other half," said Carlotta. "Your other half completes you."
"And Socrates?"
"The feeling?" asked Sage. "The loving?"
"I think you're right. The state of loving itself. For Socrates, the other per-son reminds you where to look, namely at your own capacity for love. The other does not fulfill you; your loving fulfills you. To feel loved, you must love. Does that sound right to you?"**

Notes
*   "Plato, *"The Symposium,"* 210."
** Albert Low, *The Butterfly's Dream: In Search of the Roots of Zen* (Rutland, VT: Charles E. Tuttle Company, Inc., 1993), 125–127.

Continue the discussion, keeping in mind that students should understand not only the initial attraction, but how to build relationships.

"We will soon study the psychologist Carl Jung. Jung theorized that, when you are attracted to someone, you project onto the other person what you had lost or neglected in yourself while growing up. This creates a fascina-tion, the sense of the other person as a soul-mate. When you love, you try to recapture what was lost. This is what initially brings two people together. But the other person only reflects back to you what you yourself seek. In order to find the qualities you have denied, you must look for them in yourself."[17] Ask students:

• "From where does the perception of the other as having the qualities you deny come from?"
• "Did anyone ever expect you to be someone other than who you are? Or did you ever expect someone you liked to be one way—and then you find they

are someone very different? What do you do then? Do you open the door, or do you slam it shut?"

• The crucial question is—"Can you let someone you love be who they are, not your fantasy of them? And if you do, how does that affect your relationship—and affect you psychologically?"

Ask students to reflect on what was discussed in class. "How can you apply the discussion to your own life? Did we go wrong anywhere or miss something? And fill in your chart on the components of love."

NOTES

1. Paul Ekman with Daniel Goleman, "Knowing Our Emotions, Improving Our World," *Wired To Connect: Dialogues on Social Intelligence*, More Than Sound Productions, 2007.

2. Matthieu Ricard, *Altruism: The Power of Compassion To Change Yourself And The World* (New York: Little, Brown and Company, 2015), 252.

3. Stefan G. Hofmann, PhD, Paul Grossman and Devon E. Hinton, "Loving-Kindness and Compassion Meditation: Potential for Psychological Interventions," *Clinical Psychological Review*, November 31, 2011, 1126–1132, accessed March 2, 2016. doi: 10.1016/j.cpr.2011.07.003. See also, "Compassion: Why Practice Compassion?" *Greater Good: The Science of a Meaningful Life*, accessed April 1, 2016, http://greatergood.berkeley.edu/topic/compassion/definition.

4. Ramachandran, *The Tell-Tale Brain*, 121

5. Ibid., 128.

6. Ibid., 124–5.

7. Ken Wilber, *No Boundary: Eastern and Western Approaches to Personal Growth* (Boston: Shambhala, 1985), 24–25.

8. Ramachandran, *The Tell-Tale Brain*, 128–131.

9. Ibid., 124.

10. Tania Singer, "Empathy and the Interoceptive Cortex," In *Caring Economics: Conversations on Altruism and Compassion, Between Scientists, Economists, and the Dalai Lama*, ed. Tania Singer and Mattieu Ricard (New York: Picador, 2015), 28.

11. Ibid., 29.

12. Ricard, *Altruism*, 56–64.

13. Roger Walsh, M. D., PhD, *Essential Spirituality: The 7 Central Practices to Awaken Heart and Mind* (New York: John Smiley & Sons, 1999), 107.

14. Harlow's Studies on Dependency in Monkeys, uploaded by Michael Baker, 12/16, 2010, https://www.youtube.com/watch?v=OrNBEhzjg8I

15. Spencer R. Rathus, *Essentials of Psychology, 5th Edition* (Fort Worth, Texas: 1997), 464–465. See also Susan Pinker, *The Village Effect: How Face-to-Face Contact Can Make Us Healthier, Happier, Smarter* (New York: Spiegel & Grau, 2014), 142.

16. Plato, "The Symposium," in *The Dialogues of Plato*, eds. Justin Kaplan and Benjamin Jowett (New York: Washington Square Press, 1963), 188–192.

17. M. Esther Harding, *The I and the Not I: A Study in the Development of Consciousness* (Princeton, NJ: Princeton University Press, 1965), 113–116.

Chapter 5

Compassionate Critical Thinking
Is a Process of Mindful Questioning

This chapter will attempt to make explicit what previously in the book was mostly implicit. What is critical thinking? What is the role of mindfulness, compassion, and emotion in such thinking? And what practices and insights will further help you teach it?

The prefrontal cortex, the newest and "most human" area of the brain, connects not only several areas of the cortex but also the emotional and reptilian brains. It can integrate and link together all these areas.[1] Critical thinking necessitates the ability to hold something in attention, to form complex representations and insights, map our own mental processes, attune to others, soothe fear, etc. all of which the prefrontal makes possible.[2] Mindfulness practice strengthens the prefrontal. The process of critical thinking described in this book uses mindfulness to foster the natural integrative functions of the human brain. It entails bringing awareness of feeling into thinking.

Often, students espouse what they fear might be true or what peers or family believe and not them. They want to test the idea without fully adopting it themselves, and they want you or other students to argue them free of it. When you discuss love, for example, students might say it is an illusion not because they believe it is, but because they fear it is. It is safer to say that love doesn't exist than to feel they will never achieve it. Mindful and compassionate questioning can uncover and free you from such painful and limiting beliefs and thought processes and help integrate new, deeper ways to think and live.

LESSON TWENTY-TWO: QUESTIONING—AND BEGINNING THE PROCESS OF CRITICAL THINKING

Resources for Discussion

• Daniel Goleman, *Emotional Intelligence*, 78–95.
• Bell Hooks, *Teaching Critical Thinking: Practical Wisdom* (New York: Routledge, 2010), 7–11.

What is critical thinking? Is it simply higher order thinking—evaluating the appropriateness of evidence, the truth of propositions, and the soundness of arguments? The thesis of this book is that understanding is enhanced through applying a process of active inquiry. Socratic questioning, guided by mindfulness, empathy, imagination, and self-reflection, yields a deeper, more compassionate form of critical thinking.

Sonia Nieto points out education needs to begin with what the students bring to the classroom, including their experiences and questions. To teach questioning, inquiry must be initiated not only by teachers but also by students, and so students can be allowed to suggest the starting and follow-up questions in a class discussion. "The curriculum in schools is at odds with the experiences, backgrounds, hopes, and wishes of many students."[3] New material needs to be tied to what is familiar so that students can relate to it, but without limiting it to the familiar. In teaching about classical Athens, for example, you might liken the foreign policy of Pericles to US foreign policy or to a school yard, to make it familiar, yet the differences make the subject mysterious and intriguing.

Educator Kieran Egan[4] and others say critical thinking is a dialectical process. Socrates used dialectical questioning to first uncover what you don't know about a subject, and then learn what you do know. It is a process of subjecting ideas, theories, and understandings to contrasting explanations that challenge and bring out depths of meaning and synthesize new, increasingly sophisticated, general schemes of explanation and understanding.

Dialectical can also imply a process of social analysis, interaction, and discussion, in this case one that is sincere, incisive, empathic, and noncompetitive. The perspective, knowledge, and feelings of each group member are valued.

Ask students if they believe critical thinking is important. Students' answers are often contradictory. On the one hand, students may say the world is in desperate need of critical thinking. They point to a lack of reason in politics, to inequities of the social order, racism, and sexism, to the fact that everyone seems to passionately think they are in sole possession of the one and only truth. On the other hand, many have lost the natural appreciation of an intellectual challenge that they had as children. They experience thinking only as work and not as intellectual play.

"What mental process can you use to find an answer or solution to a complex question or problem? How do you resolve disputes about what the 'correct' answer is?" These questions will drive the lesson.

The Practice

"Take a moment to get yourself settled on the edge of your chair, back straight but not rigid, eyes closed or almost closed. Let your breath settle and mind calm. Turn your attention to your breath, especially the point where the air passes over your upper lip. As you breathe in, feel the air passing over your upper lip. As you exhale, feel the air leaving. Allow your attention to calmly yet intently focus on the feeling of air coming in and going out."

Pause and allow students to practice this for a few minutes.

"With your next inhalation, breathe in a memory or image of a time you used critical thinking. Maybe you successfully figured out a solution to a problem or completed an intellectual project. Maybe something was going wrong and you righted it. Or you had a deep moral or philosophical question and you found an answer or had an insight. Just picture or feel it. What was the situation? What was the question or project? What words, thoughts or images come up for you about this endeavor?"

Pause for a few seconds. When you begin again, allow some quiet between each question. "How did you begin to answer the question or start the project? What did you feel as you began? What challenges or doubts did you face? Once you made clear what the problem or question was and how to begin, what did you do next? How did you stay on track and handle confusions or setbacks? Did your emotions help or interfere with the process—or both? How did you know and test if you were on the right track?" Pause.

"How did it feel to successfully complete the task? Just sit for a moment with the sense of successfully finding an answer or completing an intellectual challenge."

Ring the bell, and then ask students to describe in their journal the steps they went through in completing the visualized challenge. Give them a few minutes.

Then ask, "How was the practice?" Listen and discuss student responses. Follow-up questions include:

• If students ask "Why focus on the upper lip?" In response, ask: "What happened when you centered your attention on the air passing over your upper lip? Did the exercise help you focus?" The practice of pinpointed attention on an object can strengthen your ability to focus and let go of distracting thoughts. When it's possible, help students answer their own questions. Teach students to recognize when they are an authority, as in analyzing their own feelings and responses to a situation, and when they are not, as in assuming they fully understand another person's motivation—or a subject not studied extensively.

- "What kinds of challenges did you imagine in the visualization?" Students might respond with anything from fixing a bike, writing a poem, to choosing what college to attend.
- "What are the characteristics that make thinking 'critical'? When you hear the word, what comes to mind?"

Students often mention thinking rationally, using and evaluating evidence, not getting too emotional but being objective. Many will think it dry and not very creative. Some will claim that critical thinking requires creativity and maybe creativity requires critical thinking. Where is the border between the two? Is there a difference between insight derived from the creative process and the answer uncovered by critical thinking? One student answered, *"I think of critical thinking as thinking for myself."*[5]

"How do you define *critical*?" Students can take out a dictionary or their phones and find several meanings. *Critical* comes from the Greek *kritikos* meaning "able to discern," and *krinein*, "to discern, separate." Meanings can include the tendency to find fault as well as careful analysis and objective judgment.

When students feel safe and trusted, they trust their own ability and put attention and energy into thinking and questioning. They can be truly insightful. The discussion usually reveals two important aspects of critical thinking. One is being logical and reasonable; the second is determining if, or to what degree, what you say is true. "Logical" means that whatever conclusion you come to follows clearly from the premises, statements and evidence you use. The word for logical reasoning is "valid." Write the following on the chalk or whiteboard:

All humans are bipedal
George is human
Therefore, Rover is bipedal.

Then turn to the class and ask:

- "Can you logically claim, with this argument, *Rover is bipedal*? Why?"
- "Are valid arguments necessarily true?"

An argument that is both true and valid is called "sound." Write "valid" on the board and underneath it put "valid + true = sound." A student may respond with something like this:

- *But what do you mean by "truth?" Too many people claim they know the truth. There is no truth, just like there is no objective judgment. All my judgments are created by my mind, so they are biased by my mind, my likes or dislikes.*
- *Truth is whatever we decide it is.*

Student questions such as these are not a distraction from the curriculum but at the heart of it. "What is meant by *truth*?" is one of the most essential questions for any class to consider. Essential questions can't be answered by just *yes* or *no*. They are multifaceted, deep, and/or broad in scope, provoke inquiry, and are real to the students.[6] When relevance is added to trust, a classroom comes truly alive.

Students who argue there are no truths might also claim there are no facts. Ask students "What are the differences, if there are any, between a fact, a theory and an opinion? What are examples of each?" In principle, a fact is something you can verify and support and other people, in a position to do so, can also verify. A theory is not a fact but a hypothesis and way to organize facts. An opinion is a statement of your likes and dislikes. You do not have to prove that you like ice cream or that green is your favorite color. You do need supportive evidence to argue for or against global warming.

When leading a discussion, you might feel on stage or on display. This can be a very vulnerable position. Notice your response to student questions or to any classroom behavior. Instead of taking student questions or behavior as a judgment or threat to your authority, take it as a sign of where the student is, at that moment, and weave that understanding into the lesson. Ask yourself if you are reacting to student comments with judgmental comments of your own.[7] This takes commitment, care, honesty, and empathy. To teach critical thinking you must commit to thinking critically and compassionately yourself. Ask students:

- "How can we answer your question about the meaning of truth, or if there is such a thing as 'truth'?" Mindfulness, or "getting their heads clear," might be considered the beginning of the process. One meaning of critical thinking could be clear thinking.
- "Is the question clear? If not, what terms need to be defined before a discussion can begin?"
- "What happens to a discussion when the people involved use different meanings for central terms?"
- "What is the next step after clarifying the terms and meaning of the question?" The student visualizations of successfully completing a challenge usually include being "immersed" in it. You need to dive in and study diverse material relevant to the question.

When students are passionate about a question, there are several strategies and questions you can use to engage meaningful and reflective discussion. You can ask:

- "What views other than your own are consistent with the evidence?"
- "What didn't you consider? Name possible holes in your argument."
- "How do you feel when you hear a view opposite your own?"
- "Summarize what you heard from the previous speaker before you respond."

"Mistakes" or "failures" in reasoning need to be accepted as part of the critical thinking process. Ask students: "What happens if thinking is shaped by a fear of making a mistake?" When a mistake is noticed, instead of interpreting it as a cause for guilt or as a threat, take it as a signal to go in another direction. Treat the recognition of a mistake like the golden moment in mindfulness practice, as a necessary part of thinking, a moment of awakening to what is missing, and an opportunity to learn. Mindfulness helps you to more easily discern what you already know and where knowledge is needed.

Ask students:

- "Maybe you mean something different by 'truth' than I do. What does 'truth' mean to you?"
- "Is something that is true always true, in all situations?"
- "What is an example of a truth? Are there different types of truth?"
- "The boiling point of water is a scientific truth. Is the boiling point of water always the same? Does water boil at the same temperature on the equator, at sea level, as it does in the Himalayas? Does salt water boil at the same temperature as fresh water?"
- "If the boiling point of water depends on context and conditions, does that mean there is no such thing as a truth? And, if so, what is the role of mind in truth? In what ways is the truth you perceive dependent on the mind that knows?"

Truth can also be defined as what is real or what accurately corresponds with the facts. It requires clear observation. The Old English root *is treowth* or "faithfulness," which is also the source of *troth* as in *betrothed*. Parker Palmer, a teacher, author, and education activist, said: "To know in truth is to enter into the life of that which we know and to allow it to enter into ours. Truthful knowing weds the knower and the known."[8] In a good discussion, revealing hidden depths in the question leads to uncovering hidden depths in the questioners.

How could you illustrate Palmer's point about truth? In a psychology class, you might say: "We will be talking about Sigmund Freud soon. When you study Freud, try to understand his whole way of thinking, and 'see through his eyes,' or the eyes of his theory. You need empathy. Even if you don't actually agree with much of what Freud said, be able to discuss his theories as if they were your own—until you discuss critiques of his theory. When you understand, the other becomes you. In this way feeling, or empathy, can help thinking." Allow students a moment to think about and question this.

The discussion of truth can be more complex than at first imagined. For example, when a student says, *"There is no such thing as truth,"* he or she might actually be saying, *"It is the truth that there is no such thing as truth."* Or: *"I want there to be truths, but not ones I can't grasp."* It is important to hear as fully as possible what each person says, and means.

Ask the class to summarize what you have uncovered so far about the process of critical thinking. First, you settle and center your mind. You define and clarify the question, in this case, what "truth" means to you. After thoroughly researching the topic, you formulate your own or explicate someone else's theory or potential answer. "Did you ever notice how sometimes you have no idea what you feel or think about something? But once someone makes a suggestion, you immediately know if you agree or disagree?"

Once you make a choice or formulate a theory, you can evaluate it and move more quickly to understanding. You apply dialectical questioning, from the Greek *dialektike*, meaning "the art of conversation or debate."[9] You subject your thesis to questions about meaning, implications, accuracy and reasoning. You take on a different viewpoint as if it was your own and contrast it with your original, to reveal the limitations and positive points of both. You then synthesize all that you learned into a new, deeper or more inclusive theory. In this way you continuously expand your perspective.

Throughout the process, you feel empathy for the subject studied and the subject studying. Critical thinking is not, as Sonia Nieto points out, just about "higher order thinking skills in math and science as disconnected from a political awareness" but about developing "a consciousness of oneself as a critical agent in learning and transforming one's reality."[10]

The conclusions you formulate need to be stated and supported as clearly and completely as possible. But once you do so, remember to hold those conclusions with a little humility. A new day might mean new information and perspectives.

LESSON TWENTY-THREE: HOW DOES INNER SILENCE ASSIST THINKING?

Reading for Class Discussion

- Satish Kumar, *The Buddha and the Terrorist* (Chapel Hill, NC: Algonquin Books, 2004), 1–30.

In the novel, *The Buddha and the Terrorist*, based on a possibly real incident that happened 2500 years ago, the historical Buddha stops a mass murderer from terrorizing an area in ancient rural India. The man, Angulimala, is not pushing a religious or political agenda but is killing for more personal reasons. Satish Kumar, the author of the novel, is an environmental and nuclear disarmament activist, editor, educator as well as author. Students repeatedly ask to learn how to stop hurtful thoughts. Learning how to stop your own violent or hurtful thoughts and impulses can help you understand how to intervene in the violence of others.

Tell the class: "Today, the lesson will be on how the Buddha, according to legend, stops a terrorist. Then we will apply that discussion to better understand how we can use critical thinking to decrease or end violence and suffering, for ourselves and others."

The Practice

"To answer this question, let's begin by focusing attention on your own awareness. Take a moment, and allow your mind and body to calm and settle. Let your attention go to your breath, to the inhalation, then the exhalation. One moment, one breath, at a time. Feel or hear each breath, how it arises and how it dissipates. Allow yourself to be with each sensation, and each thought or image that arises. Thoughts come and go just like breath comes in and goes out. A thought might be about the future; you can label it 'future thought.' Or it can be worry, so label it 'worry thought.' Or it can be about something you need to do, so label it 'to-do thought.' Or just label it 'thought.' Simply listen and name what occurs. Do that for a few moments."

"In between the thoughts, notice a sense of calm and quiet, a silent gap. Notice whatever arises, so your mental space is the arising, the disappearing into silence and the letting go. Nothing else. Just an inhalation or arising, the gap, and then the exhalation or dissipation. Whatever arises, dissolves. If any thought arises, notice it arising. Then notice the quiet gap, then the exhalation. Do that on your own for a minute or so. As you notice the silent gap in thinking, your breath, and your mind, will calm. Sit for a moment in that calm silence."

Ring the bell.

Ask students to write about the practice of noticing the arising, the gap, and passing of thought. Then open the class for discussion by asking for questions about the practice. It is, at first, difficult to even notice thoughts. One purpose served by labeling is to highlight the thoughts so that you can notice and let them go. It takes practice. If you watch for a particular result, you often create thoughts of a watcher for that result.

- "The novel might help us understand how to deal with thoughts. How does the Buddha treat Angulimala and stop his violence?"
- "Why doesn't the Buddha fear this man who has killed so many people?"
- "For what reasons is the Buddha not afraid to die?"
- "What do you remember from our earlier discussion about what triggers fear?"

Fear is an emotion created by stories we tell ourselves about the future. The Buddha is focused on the present, so there's no such story and he can meet Angulimala straight on, with honesty. Instead of turning his back on Angulimala, he befriends him. He calls out his name and goes directly to meet him. This startles Angulimala.

- "The Buddha says, 'When you kill, you kill none other than your-self. . .Whatever you do to me you do to yourself.'[11] What does this mean to you? In what ways does Angulimala kill himself when he kills others?"
- "Why does Angulimala kill?"

Students readily reply that he is filled with hate over how he was treated as an untouchable. He is also angry at his father's sense of impotence to change the world.

"Remember, it is not just what happens that triggers a response but how you interpret it, and what beliefs you hold about human nature. What beliefs about human nature does Angulimala hold? How does Angulimala think of others?"

Angulimala treats people like objects, things to use for his own purposes, or as prey. The Buddha acts differently not only due to his character but due to what he thinks is true. He thinks anyone can change; even Angulimala, the murderer, is capable of compassion and love.

Angulimala thinks that power comes only by killing or by controlling others. The Buddha says, "I stopped desiring to control and dominate people, but you think freedom lies in killing and overpowering others. True stopping is to stop interfering in other people's lives for your own ends."[12] The power over others is dependent on their weakness. Instead, you need "power over yourself, which brings out everyone's strength."[13]

"How can you apply this to yourself? Did you ever feel pain in your-self, but instead of facing it, you yell at others? Instead of facing your own inner reality, you attack others?" If you try to control the world instead of controlling yourself, you constantly feel frustrated, depressed, or out of control. Controlling yourself is more difficult and meaningful than control-ling others.

- "How do you compassionately respond to thoughts you think are evil or wrong? How do you walk toward evil?"
- "What exactly do you think is wrong—the act your thought encourages, or the fact that you have the thought at all? Or both?"
- "Do you think having a thought marks you? If you have a violent thought, for example, does that mean you are violent?"
- "Do you think there is anyone here who has not had violent or 'wrong' thoughts? Or had just one violent thought once?"
- "Maybe you also have loving and peaceful thoughts. Do your thoughts constantly change? In which case, which thought are you?"
- "Does it surprise you to think you can stop uncomfortable thoughts by befriending them?"
- "Can you feel the violence in a thought? Do you act on a thought when it feels hurtful to you? Right there is the clue. Look to the tone or feeling of thought to understand if you should act on it or not."
- "Can you stop what you don't perceive or feel? If you face the thoughts, you can refuse to act on them. The act is what's wrong. By noticing the discomfort, you are actually quite brave."

To question and stop thoughts, you need awareness of the discomfort they bring, and you need to tolerate that awareness. Angulimala suffered not just from hurt but delusion. His delusion was in believing that his whole identity was about ending evil and projecting the source of his pain exclusively on to someone or something external to him. His own sense of powerlessness was the most powerful evil. He did not recognize his part in his suffering.

"Be gentle with yourself. Mind is naturally creative. Having thoughts is part of having a mind. It is information flowing through mind so awareness can deal with it."

Students, often without naming what they do, want to know how to act ethically. They push the class to consider ethical questions. Is ethics built on empathy for the suffering of others? On laws and norms, judging evil versus good?[14] On meeting one's own truth directly? Or on something else?

"What can you do when you're uncertain and have no idea how to answer a question? Or you're angry and want to gain some clarity?"

You can take a step back, get out of the situation for a while, take a breath or sleep on it. Sleep and dreaming gives your brain a chance to integrate material, to select what to remember and what to forget. Before you go to bed, turn off your phone. Write down, using the ancient technology of a pen and paper, a question that is on your mind. Breathe gently. And sleep. In thinking critically, once you've clarified the question and immersed yourself in different theories and possible answers, you need time to process all that information and make it yours. Your brain needs silence, a gap, so it can stop hearing old explanations and meanings long enough for new ones to arise.

The following is a summary of methods to intervene in a thought. When you notice a thought, you might imagine that there are only two "opposing" directions you can take. You might imagine all you can do is:

1. Believe and identify with the story or explanation of reality you tell your-self. You get stuck in it as if the story was about the "real" you. Or:
2. Repress it. Sometimes, an event or thought is too painful to face right away, and repression might be needed. However, when you repress some-thing, it does not just disappear. In order to say "no" to it, you keep it alive.

Neither of these strategies is very helpful. There is a middle between them, in which you remain aware but identify with neither option.

1. Question thoughts. Analyze whether the thought presents a realistic inter-pretation of the situation you are in or thinking about. We often respond to thoughts as messages to take literally when often they are more like artifacts to examine.
2. Observe with sky-like spaciousness. Openly allow thought to be in your awareness and to pass from awareness. Create a "gap" in response to a thought or inner pressure. For example, when you feel anger, instead of acting on the emotion, take deep breaths or exercise. Take a break, a walk in the woods, play a game, or sleep on a problem. Notice and enter the silence between thoughts.
3. Use what Buddhism calls an antidote. When you have fearful thoughts, think of someone who is brave. When you feel greedy, think about gen-erosity. When angry, compassionately imagine what the person you were angry at was feeling. The more you practice compassion, the more com-passion will readily arise in you.

LESSON TWENTY-FOUR: THE ROLE OF SELF-REFLECTION IN COMPASSIONATE CRITICAL THINKING

Resource

• Linda Trichter Metcalf, PhD and Tobin Simon, PhD, *Writing the Mind Alive: The Proprioceptive Method for Finding Your Authentic Voice* (New York: Random House, 2002), 22–49.

After students enter and seat themselves, you might ask:

- "What is self-reflection?"
- "There are many practices and types of self-reflection. Which, if any, do you find helpful in clarifying thinking?"

Students are asked in many schools to reflect on a project, presentation, or their overall work in a class. But how can you reflect if you don't know how to monitor thoughts and feelings moment by moment or don't know strategies for appropriately making what's unconscious conscious? If you don't know how to sit with discomfort, how can you reflect on what is uncomfortable? Without an education in progressively bringing awareness to your own mental and emotional processes, reflection is limited if not empty.

The Practice

Today's practice will be with a writing meditation. The first day you teach this practice, reserve most of a class period just for the practice and follow-up discussion. The practice is based on proprioceptive writing developed by Linda Trichter Metcalf and Tobin Simon, and described in *Writing The Mind Alive: The Proprioceptive Method for Finding Your Authentic Voice.*

"Today, we're going to use writing to help clear the mind and let your inner voice speak. Did you ever wish writing could be a mindfulness practice or a form of reflection? Can you imagine using writing to get answers to important questions and get centered?"

To some degree, many students will already be using journals or other forms of writing to do this. Build on this. Any form of writing, not only journals but short stories, poems, music lyrics as well as other art forms, are a way for students to imaginatively explore possible identities or better understand the issues and questions created by their lives.

"This writing practice enables you to make conscious material that before was unclear or hidden, and then integrate it. The full technique of proprioceptive writing takes about twenty-five minutes. The practice we will do today will take about ten minutes. The longer practice includes reading what you wrote aloud to the whole group. To listen to someone share this form of writing might be the closest you will ever come to stepping inside someone else's mind."

"In this exercise today, you will do the writing and only step inside your own mind. You can read it out loud to yourself at home. By reading what you have written out loud to yourself, you can hear your words more fully and with more psychological resonance then you do when silently reading. You can use this technique for several purposes: to answer a question or reflect on something that happened or will happen. You can use it to let go of something that plagues you or better understand a concept, or figure out how to write a paper, story or poem."

"The technique is called proprioceptive writing. *Proprio* means 'your own,' *ception* is 'sensing yourself in space and time.' In this case, you use writing to sense your inner orientation. Play music in the background to set off this moment 'as a time and place in which to establish intimacy with yourself'.[15] The teachers of this technique recommend Bach and other Baroque music, as research indicates it assists thinking."

"Pay attention to your thoughts as you do in a mindfulness practice. But instead of simply listening or feeling and letting go, as we usually do, write down whatever you hear. If you hear some great insight—write it. If you hear 'write this down,' write 'write this down.' If you feel something, write it. The object of the exercise is write what you hear and listen to your mind speak. Don't force anything. If you think there is something you 'should' be writing— put the should on the page. Treat anything said or felt as material to record."

"One other crucial instruction, which requires patience: whenever you feel or think that something you wrote is rich in unstated material and there is more there to be explored, say to yourself: 'What did I mean by that?' And write, 'What did I mean by ___?' Then write whatever comes up next in your mind. No short cuts, no editing. After the music ends, the last question will be: 'What thoughts were heard but not written?' And, 'How or what do you feel now?' Then, write, for another minute, what you hear and listen to what you write. Any questions?"

"Now, to get started, write down a question or concern. It might involve an assignment, which puzzles you, or something vague in your mind that you want to bring to light, or were wondering about when you entered the room. Write just one phrase or sentence."

Let students write for about 30 seconds.

"Now, for a few seconds just sit quietly, mindfully aware of your breath. Once the music begins, you begin. Use what you wrote as your writing prompt for the next 8 minutes. Put the pen to the page and write. The prompt is an opening of your mind. Keep it open by letting your writing be your mind speaking directly. Write whatever you hear in yourself and listen to what you write. Have fun."

As the music starts, both you and your students, quietly but energetically, write.

After 8 minutes, turn off the music and ask the class: "What thoughts were heard but not written? Maybe a thought went by too fast or you couldn't capture every word you heard. Write what you hear. Listen to what you write. How do you feel now?" Give them a minute more to write.

After a minute, ask, "How did it go?" Some will continue to write as you talk.

Many students, especially those who enjoy writing diaries or fiction, will enjoy proprioceptive writing and find it fits their interest in writing. Some will find this practice better than almost all the other techniques. Others will say that their thoughts were going too fast to keep up. Share with them: "Just remember: write what you hear. Thoughts slow down as you become focused and aware."

Make clear to yourself and your students that writing like this is different than other course work and honor this commitment. It is not to be graded. It is not a performance and is not to be critiqued like a story or essay. It's certainly not about judging your writing according to other people's standards of "good" writing. It is your inner voice speaking. It is simply a mirror of you in that moment. It is about hearing, and improving your ability to hear.[16]

If a student reports that something came up that worried him or her, ask how that student is now. "When a worry comes up, write exactly what you hear and listen to what you say. It takes practice." Check in with the student after class.

If students are unsure when to ask the proprioceptive question, "What did I mean by____?" tell them: "Ask the question when something comes up in the corner of your mind that you can barely hear. When you feel you have missed something, or you feel 'What was that about?' Or when you feel something powerful moving through you. Just asking the question is itself important as it focuses attention and wakes you up."

Then move on to questions about self-reflection: "What is the role of self-reflection in critical thinking?" Richard Paul and Linda Elder said, "Critical thinking is, in short, self-directed, self-disciplined, self-monitored, and self-corrective thinking."[17] It requires reflection and standards for thinking in order to improve thinking. Standards might include clarity, accuracy, relevance, depth, breadth, logic, and fairness.[18]

Reflection means mirroring or "bending back." You make conscious both what you're thinking as well as your idea of yourself as a thinker. You can't evaluate the quality of the process without having an idea of the capabilities of the thinker. You can pull back from an aspect of your life in order to put it into words and examine it. Thus, the question "Who is it who is thinking?" or "Who am I?" arises to some degree with each reflection.

Before adolescence, reflection is difficult. Young children readily internalize other people's views of who they are. They have difficulty reflecting on their own, stepping back from who they think they are. They are too dependent. Their need for protection, love, and support from others is too strong and they become, to some degree, a being they think others would love.

"Identification is like a glue by which consciousness attaches itself to contents of consciousness," says psychologist John Welwood. It creates a sense that this image of a self that you hold exists in the world. It says, "This is me." When you reach adolescence, you begin to free yourself from older, unconscious identifications, and more consciously direct your life and choices. Self-reflection is thus crucial for personal as well as academic success. The key to unlock the door of self-control is mindful self-reflection.

This meaning of reflection is based on memory. If you reflect on an action you took in the past, or your work over a period of time, you rely on memory. But, "What is a memory? How do memories work?" Most likely, students will describe a memory as something like a file in a filling system, as stable, unchanging. They will consider a personal memory as a pillar of their identity, even sacrosanct.

Ask students if they ever forgot something or ever noticed different people having different memories of an event. Neuroscientists say there is substantial evidence that memories change; that every time you bring up a memory, the moment of remembering becomes part of what is remembered.[19] The memory, the person remembering it, and the situation in which you retrieve it, are interdependent.

This sets up a new series of questions.

- "If a memory, like everything else in the universe, changes, how can you rely on it?"
- "There are no unchanging objects. So, what is always there for you?"
- "Besides being in the classroom, where are you right now? Where does the thread of feeling ultimately guide you?"

"It guides you to the moment you feel and think, or to the act of thinking or feeling. It guides you here, now. You step out of abstraction and find this moment.[20] Instead of focusing solely on the memory, you can focus on the whole situation in which you remember. Or you can focus on the quality of mind and feeling that is being experienced now, whether it is engaged and open versus bored and distracted. Although everything changes, you can be aware in each moment you live. This awareness is what makes any reflection, thinking, creating possible."

Ask students to summarize what they understood from the discussion of self-reflection. You might contrast two basic meanings of reflection. One is more conceptual (although not exclusively so) and one more experiential. In the first, you use concepts to step out of unconscious patterns of thought. You define and analyze. You think back, remember your process of thinking and give it voice, as in the journal questions illustrated in this book.

After solving a problem or completing a task, you and your students can self-assess by responding to open-ended questions like: "What was the process you used to solve this problem? How do you know your solution is a solution?" And specific questions: "Did you check on the reliability of your sources?" Scoring rubrics can give students a consistent set of criteria to evaluate their work. They also tell students what the teacher values.

The second meaning of reflection is the self-awareness exemplified by mindfulness—a direct, open, consciousness of what you are aware of now. You don't need to put what you think and feel into words; that will happen soon enough. You only need to feel and notice it.

With mindfulness, you focus on an object; then you take in the whole context. You take in the world from the perspective of whatever is observed or considered; and then you take in your unique response and personal perspective. To the degree that it's possible, you know the observed in relation to you. And then you know yourself in relation to the observed. This dynamic shifting of perspectives, you and other, object and context, makes whatever is observed come alive. Reflective awareness turns learning course material into learning about you. Your mind becomes more fluid and you learn more proficiently.

A Simple Practice and Technique for Examining Your Solution or Conclusion

If you have just completed an assignment, written an essay, or solved a problem, reflect on your work and test your solution. Sit silently for a moment. Take three breaths. Once your mind and body are settled, open your eyes and slowly examine your work. Use feeling, reason, and imagination. Ask yourself questions like:

- "Where does the work feel *right*? Where does it feel *off*?"
- When you look at lines in an essay that feel *off*, consider: "What did I mean by this? What did I mean to say that I didn't say?"
- "Did I answer the whole question or leave anything out?"
- "If this is true, then what?" Engage the imagination to discern the implications or consequences of a solution or conclusion.

And listen for your answers. Or write down in simple words what you want to say or think the answer is. If you can't, your understanding has not ripened. If the Buddha can befriend Angulimala, you can befriend your own mind.

When you teach students the writing process, make the point that creating or understanding requires different brain processes than editing for grammar. For example, you might use visual processing areas of the brain to picture a scene in writing a story, but use the hippocampus and left temporal language areas for recording what you've visualized.[21] If you try to understand, create, and edit all at once, your mind wars with itself. Use incubation periods to let the mind settle. Use brainstorming techniques to let your mind free and to separate working on mechanics from creative thinking. Proprioceptive writing is an excellent way to brainstorm. When students know the process of critical thinking, are engaged by the task, and feel supported by the teacher, they will more easily create insight and understanding.

When you are mindful, instead of integrating thought and feeling into a full emotion, you can integrate mind and heart into insight. Mindfulness gives you the training you need to work with your mind, not against it, so you can think clearly and be fully present with whomever you are with, or whatever concept you are trying to understand. It gives your mind the support it needs both to create and to think clearly. The following summarizes this supportive process.

The Natural Process of Compassionate Critical Thinking

1. Mental Preparation: Conceptual Knowing and Immersion in the Question.
   a. Focus awareness. Define, clarify and engage with the question. Use mindfulness and other practices to inquire into what exactly is the problem or question. What do you know? What do you need to learn?
   b. Immerse yourself in the query. Research, collect material evidence, imagine possible explanations, and examine diverse perspectives.
   c. Formulate your own thesis and question it. Formulate antitheses on your own or in a group, analyze the material and various answers, and consider the trustworthiness of sources, the truth of propositions, and the validity of arguments.
2. Throughout the Process, Add the Perspective of the Heart and Awareness of Feeling:
   a. Choice requires feeling as well as thinking. Deepen the engagement. Use imagination and empathy to "feel out" or inhabit the question; explore and examine possible implications and consequences of any answer.
   b. To get to new ways of understanding, you need to let go of old ones. Immersion and questioning often lead to frustration and resistance. Reflect mindfully on what you feel as you examine each possible answer, and on your process. Notice if emotions or cognitive biases distort your understanding. Do you need to step back from the material and let it sit?
   c. Integrate the material by stepping back, meditating, dreaming. Let it incubate in your mind until thinking clears and new understanding is reached.
3. Insight, Synthesis, and Application:
   a. Synthesize the new insight and create a new thesis.
   b. Translate, apply, question, and test if the new thesis works.
   c. Is more understanding needed? Do you need to reengage the process?

NOTES

1. Daniel Siegel, M. D., *Mindsight: The New Science of Personal Transformation* (New York: Bantam, 2010), 22.

2. Ibid., 8, 9.

3. Sonia Nieto, "Lessons from Students on Creating a Chance to Dream," in *Shifting Histories: Transforming Education for Social Change*, eds. Gladys Capella Noya, Kathryn Geismar, and Guitele Nicoleau (Cambridge, MA: Harvard University Press, 1995), 9.

4. Kieran Egan, *The Educated Mind: How Cognitive Tools Shape Our Understanding* (Chicago, IL: University of Chicago Press, 1997), 268.

5. For an account of critical thinking congruent with the student comment and my own approach, see Bell Hooks, *Teaching Critical Thinking*, 7–11.

6. Grant Wiggins and Jay McTighe, *Understanding By Design* (Alexandria, VA: ASCD, 1998), 20–37.

7. For more self-reflective questions, see Neil Postman and Charles Weingartner, *Teaching as a Subversive Activity: a no-holds-barred assault on outdated teaching methods—with dramatic and practical proposals on how education can be made relevant to today's world* (New York: Dell Publishing Co., 1969), 197–198.

8. Parker J. Palmer, *To Know as We Are Known: Education as a Spiritual Journey* (New York: Harper Collins, 1993), 31.

9. Simon Blackburn, *The Oxford Dictionary of Philosophy* (Oxford: Oxford University Press, 1994), 10.

10. Nieto, *Shifting Histories*, 6.

11. Satish Kumar, *The Buddha and the Terrorist* (Chapel Hill, NC: Algonquin, 2004), 14.

12. Ibid., 25.

13. Ibid., 18–20

14. See Mark Matousek, *Ethical Wisdom: What Makes Us Good?* (New York: Doubleday, 2011), 4–11, 28–31.

15. Ibid., 28.

16. Ibid., 44.

17. Linda Elder and Richard Paul, "Why Critical Thinking?" *The Critical Thinking Community*. Accessed January 22, 2016, http://www.criticalthinking.org/pages/defining-critical-thinking/766.

18. Linda Elder and Richard Paul, "Universal Intellectual Standards," *The Critical Thinking Community*. Accessed January 22, 2016, http://www.criticalthinking.org/pages/universal-intellectual-standards/527.

19. Norman Doidge, *The Brain that Changes Itself: Stories of Personal Triumph from the Frontiers of Brain Science* (New York: Penguin Books, 2007), 224–225, 378–379.

20. Welwood, "Reflection and Presence," in *Transpersonal Knowing: Exploring the Horizon of Consciousness*, ed. Tobin Hart et al. (Albany, NY: State University of New York Press, 2000), 107.

21. Carl Zimmer, "This Is Your Brain on Writing," *New York Times*, June 06, 2014, D3.

Conclusion

The calendar year, especially in a school, has a distinct rhythm to it. As you finish the last lesson, maybe it is early December and winter is closing in. Two more complete weeks and then the holidays. This period of time is full of anticipation, for a break from school, for holidays filled with feeling. Or maybe it is early spring and the first flowers are showing themselves amidst the snow, and the day is so warm that students can barely sit in their seats.

One gift that a teacher brings to students (and vice versa) is the mere fact of companionship; you live the school year together. You, the teacher, reassure students. You provide, hopefully, a secure and a caring base. You model a relationship with time and presence. How do you relate to the approaching winter? To a storm? To a freakishly warm day near the end of winter? To spring? To tests? Work? All these moments that you are together? You become family for a time. What kind of family will you be? What kind of person will you be as a teacher?

Teaching can be exhausting, maddening, and stressful. You never know for sure how or who you are influencing. Although every teacher experiences times of great doubt, you know teaching is creative and can positively impact the lives of at least most students. You might discipline a student or tell one to rewrite an essay several times and the student glares at you. You think she hates you. Ten or fifteen years later, after completing her first year teaching, she comes to visit you at school and tell you that you had turned her life around. And she isn't the only one. Such moments are priceless.

The more you use mindfulness, the better you hear what students have to say, the better they hear you. Feeling is not secondary to academics but at the heart of it. Mindfulness practice shows students that whatever arises, they can face it; the depths may be dark and scary, but every mind has, or is its own, light.

The class is a refuge for students and an example of what is possible in life. You learn from each other that it is possible to live a meaningful life. It is possible to create a supportive community. It is even probable that by creating a supportive community with others, you deepen your life. You measure success in life not with grades but more by how you are with other people.

One problem with the way critical thinking is often conceptualized and taught arises from not understanding human psychology. When a problem or question arises, you want an answer. Many people don't like the discomfort of not-knowing. Without knowing how to use, learn from, and live with discomfort, you can easily rush to make a judgment.

Instead of rushing to an answer, you need to take time to feel as well as think your way through reams of evidence and potential solutions. You can't allow a predilection for old or comforting answers to eliminate the possibility of new and more difficult, yet possibly exciting, ones. Taking the time to slow down often allows your mind the space it needs to work more skillfully.

The process of compassionate critical thinking is critical thinking, questioning, and solving problems with added benefits. It is a process that integrates not only information and logic, but also feeling and emotion. It teaches you how to live and accept yourself and all aspects of your life. It is expanding the reach of your life. It is not dry, objective, and unemotional but engaged and deeply concerned, not just with the world but as the world. You realize you can never step out of the world or be anything other than an aspect of it. You are, ultimately, the world examining itself. You teach students not only what the world is but how to break out of conditioned limits and realize what is possible. Now that is a fulfilling life.

Acknowledgments

I used to think writing a book was just about the solitary writer expressing his or her story or insights. But now I realize it takes a community to write a book. So many people helped make this book a reality.

Let me start with the students, parents, and staff of the Lehman Alternative Community School. In a way, this book is about this school. Working at the school was one of the central transformative experiences of my life. It demanded a level of commitment, creativity, and intellectual and emotional engagement I hadn't known before. Never before or since have I worked with such a dedicated and inspiring group of people.

The principal, Dr. Dave Lehman, set the tone for all of us. He directed, protected, inspired, and sometimes serenaded (with his guitar) the school. So many staff helped me out when I worked there so I can only thank a few who helped directly with this book: Sarah Jane Bokaer, Hayya Mintz, Debbie Cowell, and Linda Winters.

And so many students befriended, challenged, puzzled, and demanded more from me than I knew I could give and, if I messed up, usually gave me another chance the next day. I would like to especially thank four students who played crucial roles in making this book a reality: Susanna Siegel, Sasha Lilley, Yarra Berger, and Inge Johnson.

Other people were also wonderfully generous with their time providing valuable feedback and support: Laurie Ruben, Robert Heavner, Diane Traina, Elaine Mansfield, and Eileen Ain.

My agent, Jill Swenson, pushed, directed, and educated me about how to edit and get my book published. We went through challenging times and yet are still standing together. Without her, I doubt the book would have been published. Sarah Jubar, the acquisitions editor for Rowman and Littlefield, and her assistant, Bethany Janka, recognized the value of my book and, in a supportive and insightful way, helped shape it to be more eloquent and better equipped to speak to my audience.

Then, there are my teachers. I am going to speak only of those who had a great impact on the book. Roshi Philip Kapleau first introduced me to meditation practice. Linda Trichter Metcalf and Tobin Simon, teachers of Proprioceptive Writing, helped me revive my love of, and ability to teach, writing. David Loy, Zen Teacher and philosopher, through the many books of his I read and an intensive class, deepened my understanding of Buddhism, meditation, and the ethical responsibility we all bear one another.

And then there is Hidy Ochiai. I have studied the art of Karate-Do (and Kobudo and meditation) with him for 41 years and yet each and every class teaches me something new, about myself, as well as the art of karate. Hidy Ochiai models and redefines for me what it means to be a teacher. He shows how deep and meaningful an impact a teacher can make in a student's life and that if I want to inspire my students to reach deeply inside themselves in their studies, I have to do it first.

I would like to thank my Dad. The world would be a so much better place if everyone had a Dad who loved his children as deeply as my Dad loves my brother and me. And my wife, Linda. Wow. More than anyone else, she dives into the mysteries of life with me. When I need support, or get lost in abstractions, she centers me in the reality of others and the feel of the wind and trees. She reminds me, daily, that no matter how inspired I am, I can't eat words, and that a loving relationship is the deepest inspiration.

Thank you all.

Appendix

Further Resources

MINDFULNESS

Austin, James. *Meditating Selflessly: Practical Neural Zen*. Cambridge, MA: MIT Press, 2011.

Campbell, Emily. "Mindfulness in Education Research Highlights." *Greater Good: The Science of a Meaningful Life*. September 16, 2014. http://greatergood.berkeley. edu/article/item/mindfulness_in_education_research_highlights.

Campbell, Joseph. *The Hero With A Thousand Faces*. New York: MJF Books, 1947.

Ekman, Paul, with Daniel Goleman. "Knowing Our Emotions, Improving Our World." *Wired To Connect: Dialogues on Social Intelligence*, More Than Sound Productions, 2007.

Fanning Patrick, *Visualization for Change: A Step-By-Step Guide to Using Your Powers of Imagination for Self-Improvement, Therapy, Healing & Pain Control*. Oakland, CA: New Harbinger Publications, Inc. 1988.

Goldstein, Joseph. *Mindfulness: A Practical Guide to Awakening*. Boulder, CO: Sounds True, Inc., 2013.

Jennings, Patricia. *Mindfulness for Teachers: Simple Skills for Peace and Productivity in the Classroom*. New York: W. W. Norton & Co., 2015.

Lantieri, Linda and Daniel Goleman. *Building Emotional Intelligence: Techniques to Cultivate Inner Strength in Children*. Boulder, CO: Sounds True, 2008.

LeShan, Lawrence. *How to Meditate: The Acclaimed Guide to Self-Discovery*. New York: Bantam Books, 1974.

Neville, Bernie. *Educating Psyche: Emotion, Imagination and the Unconscious in Learning*. North Blackburn Victoria, Australia: Collins Dove, 1989.

Salzberg, Sharon. *The Force of Kindness: Change Your Life with Love and Compassion*. Boulder, CO: Sounds True, Inc., 2005.

Saltzman, Amy. *A Still Quiet Place: A Mindfulness Program for Teaching Children and Adolescents to Ease Stress and Difficult Emotions*. Oakland, CA: New Harbinger, 2014.

Wallace, Alan. *Minding Closely: The Four Applications of Mindfulness*. Ithaca, N. Y: Snow Lion Publications, 2011.

THE BRAIN

Begley, Sharon. *Train Your Mind, Change Your Brain: The Breakthrough Collaboration Between Neuroscience and Buddhism*. New York: Ballantine Books, 2007.

Davidson, Richard with Daniel Goleman. "Cultivating Emotional Skills" *Wired to Connect: Dialogues on Social Intelligence*, More Than Sound Productions. 2007.

Goleman, Daniel. *Emotional Intelligence: Why It Can Matter More Than IQ*. New York: Bantam Books, 1995.

Hanson, Rick, with Richard Mendius. *Buddha's Brain: The Practical Neuroscience of Happiness, Love, and Wisdom*. Oakland, CA: New Harbinger Publications, Inc., 2009.

Harrington, Anne and Arthur Zajonc, eds. *The Dalai Lama at MIT*. Cambridge, MA: Harvard University Press, 2006.

Hayward, Jeremy. *Letters to Vanessa: On Love, Science, and Awareness in an Enchanted World*. Boston, MA: Shambhala, 1997.

Kahneman, Daniel. *Thinking Fast and Slow*. New York: Farrar, Straus and Giroux, 2011.

Lakoff, George and Mark Johnson. *Metaphors We Live By*. Chicago: University of Chicago Press. 1980.

McGilchrist, Iain. *The Master and his Emissary: The Divided Brain and the Making of the Western World*. New Haven, CT: Yale University Press, 2009.

Metzinger, Thomas. *The Ego Tunnel: The Science of the Mind and the Myth of the Self.* New York: Basic Books, 2009.

Nataraja, Dr. Shanida. *The Blissful Brain: Neuroscience and Proof of the Power of Meditation*. London: Gaia Books, 2008.

Ramachandran, V. S. *The Tell-Tale Brain*. New York: W. W. Norton & Co., 2011.

Siegel, Daniel. *Mindsight: The New Science of Personal Transformation*. New York: Bantam Books, 2010.

Wallace, Alan. *Mind in The Balance: Meditation in Science, Buddhism, and Christianity*. New York: Columbia University Press, 2009.

EMOTIONS

Buber, Martin. *I and Thou, 2nd Edition*. New York: Charles Scribner's Sons, 1970.

Csikszentmihalyi, Mihalyi. *Flow: The Psychology of Optimal Experience*. New York: Harper Collins, 1990.

Ekman, Paul. ed. *Emotional Awareness, Overcoming the Obstacles to Psychological Balance and Compassion*. New York: Henry Holt and Company, 2008.

Ekman, Paul. *Emotions Revealed: Recognizing Faces and Feelings to Improve Communication and Emotional Life*. New York: Times Books, 2003.

Epley, Nicholas. *Mindwise: How We Understand What Others Think, Believe, Feel, and Want*. New York: Alfred A. Knopf, 2014.

Goleman, Daniel. *Social Intelligence: The New Science of Human Relationships.* New York: Bantam Books, 2006.

Hagen, Steve. *Buddhism Plain and Simple: The Practice of Being Aware, Right Now, Every Day.* New York: Broadway Books, 1998.

Hoff, Benjamin. *The Tao of Pooh.* New York: Penguin, 1982.

LeDoux, Joseph. *The Emotional Brain: The Mysterious Underpinnings of Emotional Life.* New York: Touchstone, 1996.

Leifer, Ron M. D. *The Happiness Project: Transforming the Three Poisons that Cause the Suffering We Inflict on Ourselves and Others.* Ithaca, NY: Snow Lion Press, 1997.

Lieberman, Mathew D. *Social: Why Our Brains Are Wired to Connect.* New York: Crown Publishers, 2013.

LeShan, Lawrence. *The Psychology of War: Comprehending its Mystique and its Madness.* New York: Helios Press.

Linden, David J. *Touch: The Science of Hand, Heart, and Mind.* New York: Viking, 2015.

Loy, David. *A Buddhist History of the West: Studies in Lack.* Albany, NY. SUNY Press, 2002.

———. *Money, Sex, War, Karma: Notes for a Buddhist Revolution.* Boston, MA: Wisdom Publications, 2008.

Noddings, Nel. *Happiness and Education.* New York: Cambridge University Press, 2003.

Siegel, Daniel. *The Developing Mind: How Relationships and the Brain Interact to Shape Who we Are,* 2nd *Edition.* New York: Guilford Press, 2012.

Walsh, Roger. *Essential Spirituality: Exercises from the World's Religions to Cultivate Kindness, Love, Joy, Peace, Vision, Wisdom and Generosity.* New York: John Wiley & Sons, Inc., 1999.

Williams, Mark and John Teasdale, Zindel Segal, and Jon Kabat-Zinn. *The Mindful Way through Depression: Freeing Yourself from Chronic Unhappiness.* New York: Guilford Press, 2007.

COMPASSION

Dalai Lama, *Ethics For A New Millennium.* New York: Riverhead Books, 1999.

Feldman, Christina and Jack Kornfield, eds. *Soul Food: Stories to Nourish the Spirit and the Heart.* San Francisco, CA: HarperOne, 1996.

"Compassion: Why Practice Compassion?" *Greater Good: The Science of a Meaningful Life,* accessed April 1, 2016, http://greatergood.berkeley.edu/topic/compassion/definition.This includes a video of Dacher Keltner on the Evolutionary Roots of Compassion, and one with Paul Ekman on Heroic Compassion and Altruism.

Harding, M. Esther. *The I and the Not I: A Study in the Development of Consciousness.* Princeton, NJ: Princeton University Press, 1965.

Intrator, Sam M. and Megan Scribner, ed. *Teaching with Fire: Poetry that Sustains the Courage to Teach.* San Francisco, CA. Jossey-Bass, 2003.

Keltner, Dacher and Jason Marsh, Jeremy Adam Smith, eds. *The Compassionate Instinct: The Science of Human Goodness.* New York: W. W. Norton & Company, 2010.

Low, Albert. *The Butterfly's Dream: In Search of the Roots of Zen.* Rutland, VT: Charles E. Tuttle Company, Inc., 1993.

Matousek, Mark. *Ethical Wisdom: What Makes Us Good.* New York: Doubleday, 2011.

Ricard, Mathieu. *Altruism: The Power of Compassion to Change Yourself and the World.* New York: Little Brown, 2015.

Salzberg, Sharon. *Loving-Kindness: The Revolutionary Art of Happiness.* Boston, MA: Shambhala, 1997.

Singer, Tania and Mattieu Ricard, eds. *Caring Economics: Conversations on Altruism and Compassion, Between Scientists, Economists, and The Dalai Lama.* New York: Picador, 2015.

Wilber, Ken. *No Boundary: Eastern and Western Approaches to Personal Growth.* Boston, MA: New Science Library, 1979.

CRITICAL THINKING

Blum, Lawrence. *High Schools, Race, and America's Future.* Cambridge, MA: Harvard Education Press, 2012.

Egan, Kieran. *The Educated Mind: How Cognitive Tools Shape Our Understanding.* Chicago, IL: University of Chicago Press, 1997.

Elder, Linda and Richard Paul. "Why Critical Thinking?" *The Critical Thinking Community.* Accessed January 22, 2016. http://www.criticalthinking.org/pages/defining-critical-thinking/766

"Universal Intellectual Standards." *The Critical Thinking Community.* Accessed January 22, 2016. http://www.criticalthinking.org/pages/universal-intellectual-standards/527.

Finley, Todd. "Critical Thinking Pathways." *Edutopia.* (2014). Accessed April 8, 2016. http://www.edutopia.org/blog/critical-thinking-pathways-todd-finley

Freire, Paulo. *Pedagogy of the Oppressed.* New York: Seabury Press, 1968.

Hare, William. "Open-Minded Inquiry." *The Critical Thinking Community.* Accessed April 8, 2016. http://www.criticalthinking.org/pages/open-minded-inquiry/579

Hooks, Bell. *Teaching Critical Thinking: Practical Wisdom.* New York: Routledge, 2010.

Jowett, Benjamin, trans. *Plato, Six Great Dialogues: Apology, Crito, Phaedo, Phaedrus, Symposium, and The Republic.* New York: Dover Thrift Editions, 2007.

Kramer, Gregory. *Insight Dialogue. A Buddhist Practice for Cultivating Wisdom and Compassion Through Meditation in Dialogue.* Boston, MA: Shambhala, 2007.

Metcalf, Linda Trichter and Tobin Simon. *Writing The Mind Alive: The Proprioceptive Method for Finding Your Authentic Voice.* New York: Ballantine Books, 2002.

Needleman, Jacob. *The Heart of Philosophy.* San Francisco: Harper & Row, 1986.

Nieto, Sonia "Lessons from Students on Creating a Chance to Dream" in *Shifting Histories: Transforming Education for Social Change*, eds., Gladys Capella Noya, Kathryn Geismar, and Guitele Nicoleau, 3–33. Cambridge, MA: Harvard University Press, 1995.

Palmer, Parker J. *To Know as We Are Known: Education as a Spiritual Journey.* New York: Harper Collins, 1993.

Postman, Neil and Charles Weingartner, Teaching as a Subversive Activity: *A no-holds-barred assault on outdated teaching methods—with dramatic and practical proposals on how education can be made relevant to today's world.* New York: Dell Publishing Co., 1969.

Ravitch, Diane. *Reign of Error: The Hoax of the Privatization Movement and the Danger to America's Public Schools.* New York: Alfred A Knopf, 2013.

Simon, Katherine. *Moral Questions in the Curriculum: How to Get Kids to Think Deeply About Real Life and Their Schoolwork.* New Haven, CT: Yale University Press, 2001.

Wiggins, Grant and Jay McTighe. *Understanding By Design.* Alexandria, VA: ASCD, 1998.

Index

About the Author

Ira Rabois recently retired from the Lehman Alternative Community School, a public secondary school in Ithaca, NY, where he taught English, philosophy, history, drama, karate and psychology for 27 years. He earned a B.A. from the University of Michigan, a M.A.T. from SUNY-Binghamton, and served in the Peace Corps in Sierra Leone. He has studied Zen and Japanese martial arts for 41 years with Hidy Ochiai. He took classes in meditation and Buddhist philosophy and psychology at Namgyal Institute for Tibetan Studies and the Omega Institute with David Loy, Robert Thurman, and others. He also studied healing meditation with the Consciousness Research and Training Project, and Proprioceptive Writing with Linda Trichter Metcalf and Tobin Simon. He lives with his wife, Linda, in an old apple orchard. His blog on education and mindfulness can be found at irarabois.com.

Ingram Content Group UK Ltd.
Milton Keynes UK
UKHW041810090323
418314UK00004B/35